The Narcissistic Trauma Survival Guide

A Guided Journey to Healing, Recovery, and
Restoration After Narcissistic Abuse

Graham Michaels

Palmetto Digital Media

Contents

Introduction

You have lived it: the silent treatments that left you questioning your worth, the subtle manipulations that twisted your reality, the moments of charm that suddenly turned cold. It is a form of suffering that often goes unrecognized by others, leaving you to navigate a maze of confusion and pain alone. But here, in these pages, you are understood. This book is your beacon of hope, shining a light on the path to healing from the shadows cast by narcissistic trauma.

"The Narcissistic Trauma Survival Guide: A Guided Journey to Healing, Recovery, and Restoration After Narcissistic Abuse" is more than just an exploration of narcissistic abuse. It is a practical, step-by-step guide designed to lead you out of the darkness and into a place of healing and self-reclamation. Whether you are just beginning to recognize the signs of narcissistic trauma or already on your journey to recovery, or anywhere in between, this book offers a comprehensive roadmap to empower you to reclaim your life.

Designed to guide you through the stages of understanding narcissistic trauma, breaking free, and rebuilding your life, this book is your companion in transformation. Along the way, you will find real-life stories that resonate with your experiences, practical exercises to aid your recovery, and expert advice to light your path. Each section builds on the last, creating a scaffold for your journey from target (because you *were* targeted by the narcissist) to survivor to thriver.

I, myself, have walked this path before you and I will walk it with you now.

What sets this book apart is its blend of personal insight, actionable advice, and a sincerely empathetic tone. As someone who has escaped, survived, and reclaimed myself from long-term narcissistic abuse, I have passionately dedicated my life to helping others heal, as well. I bring my profound understanding of the journey you are embarking on and decades of professional experience in Emergency Medicine and Crisis Intervention. My experiences, combined with my commitment to providing accessible, reputable guidance, have shaped this book into what I hope will be an invaluable tool for you to overcome the effects of narcissistic trauma.

As you turn these pages, I encourage you to engage actively with the material. Reflect on your experiences, complete the exercises, and allow yourself to embrace the healing process. It won't always be easy, but remember, you are not alone. This book is here to provide the support, tools, and encouragement you need to navigate your recovery.

Healing is possible. With each step forward, you move away from pain and towards a life defined by your strength, resilience, and renewal. Let this book guide you as you enter the light of your new beginning, your Life 2.0.

Together, we will embark on your journey toward healing and restoration. Your future self is waiting to thank you.

Part 1: The Anatomy of Narcissistic Trauma

In the heart of a serene, bustling city, a well-dressed individual stands out—not for the attire but for the magnetic field of charisma encircling them. With a smile that draws people in and a gaze that seems to see right through you, this person possesses an almost gravitational allure. Yet, beneath this captivating exterior lies a complex psychological construct that impacts the individual and everyone who enters their orbit. This section delves into the world as seen through the eyes of someone with narcissistic traits, unraveling the psychological fabric that constitutes narcissistic personality disorder (NPD).

> *"Beware of false prophets, who come to you in sheep's clothing but inwardly are ravenous wolves."*
> Matthew 7:15 (New International Version)

Chapter 1: The Narcissist's World

A Psychological Deep Dive

Nature of Narcissism

Narcissism, a term that stems from the Greek myth of Narcissus, who fell in love with his reflection, today signifies a complex spectrum of behaviors and traits characterized by an inflated sense of self-importance, a deep need for excessive attention and admiration, coupled with a lack of empathy for others. The Diagnostic and Statistical Manual of Mental Disorders, Fifth Edition (DSM-5), categorizes Narcissistic Personality Disorder as a pervasive pattern of grandiosity, the need for admiration, and a distinct lack of empathy. However, it's crucial to distinguish between narcissistic personality traits, which many may exhibit to varying degrees, and NPD, a clinical disorder that significantly impacts an individual's functioning.

Control and Power

At the core of the narcissist's interactions lies the primal need for control and power. This necessity stems from a deep-seated fear of vulnerability; by orchestrating the dynamics of their relationships, narcissists shield themselves from perceived threats to their self-esteem. The control manifests in various ways, from overt domination to subtle manipulation, often leaving those in their wake feeling disempowered and voiceless. The manipulation tactics can include gaslighting, where the target's reality is systematically denied and distorted, leaving them questioning their sanity and truth.

Perception of Reality

The narcissist's perception of reality is often distorted through a lens of self-interest and entitlement. This distorted view fosters unrealistic expectations from those around them, expecting unwavering compliance with their desires and demands. Such expectations are not born from a mutual understanding or empathy but from the narcissist's belief in their inherent superiority. This disparity between the narcissist's expectations and the inevitable shortcomings of reality often leads to conflicts, disappointment, and a cycle of blame directed outward, as the narcissist seldom acknowledges their role in the discord.

Impact on Targets

Living in the narcissist's world can lead to profound psychological impacts on their targets, including confusion, self-doubt, and a warped sense of reality. The constant manipulation and emotional turmoil can erode your sense of self, making it challenging to distinguish between what is real and what has been manufactured and manipulated. This psychological toll is not just limited to emotional consequences but can manifest in physical symptoms as well, such as anxiety, depression, and stress-related illnesses. Targets often find themselves in a perpetual state of trying to appease the narcissist, sacrificing their own needs and well-being in the process.

The journey through understanding the nature and impact of narcissistic behaviors is not about vilifying or excusing those with narcissistic traits but about gaining an understanding of the complex interplay between personality disorders and interpersonal relationships. It is about recognizing the signs, understanding the dynamics at play, and, most importantly, empowering those who find themselves caught in the web of narcissistic abuse to navigate their way to safety and recovery.

Chapter 2: Decoding Gaslighting

The Erosion of Reality

Gaslighting stands as one of the most insidious forms of manipulation, a tactic often employed by individuals with narcissistic tendencies to sow seeds of doubt in the mind of their target, *you*. This psychological strategy involves the deliberate attempt to skew your sense of reality, making you question your memory, perception, or sanity. The term itself originates from the 1938 stage play "Gas Light," where a husband manipulates his wife into believing she's losing her mind, a narrative that chillingly mirrors the experiences of many who've endured this form of psychological abuse.

Definition and Techniques

At its core, gaslighting is an exercise in power and control, where the abuser denies your experience, often with statements like "That never happened" or "You're imagining things." This manipulation is not random but a calculated effort to destabilize and dominate. Common techniques include:

- **Trivializing**: Making you believe your thoughts or needs are insignificant.

- **Withholding**: Pretending not to understand you or refusing to listen.

- **Countering**: Questioning your memory of events, even when you remember them accurately.

- **Blocking and Diverting**: Changing the subject or questioning your thoughts to divert the conversation from the topic.

Psychological Effects

The repercussions of gaslighting extend far beyond momentary confusion, weaving a complex tapestry of psychological turmoil. You have likely often experienced:

- **Anxiety**: A constant state of second-guessing can lead to pervasive feelings of anxiety.

- **Confusion**: Regularly questioning your reality fosters a profound sense of confusion.

- **Loss of Trust**: You start doubting your perceptions and fundamental ability to trust yourself and others.

This psychological disorientation doesn't just affect your mental health; it can ripple out, affecting relationships, job performance, and your social life, creating a pervasive sense of isolation and despair.

Strategies of Resistance

The path to resisting gaslighting and reclaiming your reality starts with awareness and is fortified by action. Here are strategies to counteract gaslighting:

- **Document Reality**: Keeping a journal of events, conversations, and how they made you feel can serve as a tangible anchor to your reality.

- **Seek External Validation**: Sometimes, talking to friends, family, or a therapist can provide an outside perspective, validating your experiences and feelings.

- **Set Boundaries**: Establishing and enforcing boundaries with the gaslighter can help protect your mental and emotional well-being.

- **Trust Your Gut**: Start cultivating trust in your instincts again; if something feels off, there's a good chance it is.

The journey to overcoming the effects of gaslighting is profoundly personal and can, at times, be a rocky path to walk, fraught with challenges. Whether you believe it at this point or not, you *do* have the strength and the power to begin, and these strategies offer a starting point for reclaiming autonomy over your perceptions and emotions.

Case Studies

To illustrate the impact of gaslighting and the effectiveness of resistance strategies, let's look at real-life examples:

1. **A Personal Relationship Scenario**: Maria began to notice discrepancies between her recollections of events and
   her partner's accounts. Over time, she felt increasingly
   anxious and doubted her memory. By keeping a journal,
   Maria documented instances of gaslighting, which she
   later discussed with a therapist. This external validation
   helped her recognize the manipulation, empowering her
   to confront her partner and ultimately decide to leave the
   relationship.

2. **A Workplace Context**: Tom experienced gaslighting
   from a supervisor who denied conversations, leading Tom
   to question his professional competence. Tom started
   emailing summaries of their meetings to his supervisor for
   "clarification" and "record-keeping," subtly documenting
   the gaslighting behavior. This not only provided Tom
   with a written record but also subtly discouraged further
   attempts at gaslighting by making the supervisor aware
   that their interactions were being documented.

These examples underscore the insidious nature of gaslighting
and the power of strategic resistance. By documenting their experiences and seeking external validation, both Maria and Tom were
able to assert their reality, paving the way for healthier interactions
and environments.

The process of overcoming gaslighting requires patience, resilience, and, often, external support. It's about slowly rebuilding

the trust in your perceptions and judgments that were eroded. While the journey may be challenging, it is also filled with opportunities for growth, self-discovery, and empowerment. Through understanding and resisting gaslighting, you can start to untangle the web of manipulation, reclaim your reality, and move forward with a renewed sense of confidence and clarity.

Chapter 3: The Cycle of Abuse

Recognizing the Patterns

Understanding the cycle of narcissistic abuse is pivotal in recognizing the patterns that define this form of manipulation and control. This cycle typically unfolds in three distinct phases: idealization, devaluation, and discard. Each phase serves a specific purpose in the narcissist's playbook, manipulating the emotions and perceptions of their targets to maintain control and feed their ego.

Phases of the Cycle

- **Idealization**: This phase is marked by excessive affection, attention, and admiration. The narcissist showers you with compliments, gifts, and promises of an ideal future together, creating a euphoric sense of connection and belonging. You may have felt that you have found your soulmate, unaware that this phase is calculated to hook your attention and affection.

- **Devaluation**: Once the narcissist feels secure in their hold over you, the tone shifts dramatically. Compliments turn to criticism, affection to indifference, or hostility. The shift is often gradual, making it difficult for you to pinpoint when or why the change occurred. The purpose here is to erode your self-esteem, making you more dependent on the narcissist's approval and affection.

- **Discard**: In the third phase, the narcissist withdraws their attention and affection, often abruptly. They may threaten to end the relationship or emotionally withdraw, leaving you feeling confused, devastated, and desperate to regain the narcissist's affection. Unfortunately, this phase is not always permanent; narcissists often cycle back to idealization if they believe they can still extract value from the relationship.

Emotional Rollercoaster

Navigating these phases can feel like riding an emotional rollercoaster. The highs of the idealization phase are intoxicating, creating a powerful bond between you and the narcissist. However, the subsequent shift to devaluation introduces profound confusion and pain as you strive to recapture the affection and approval you once received so freely. The discard phase often leaves you feeling abandoned, worthless, and alone, unsure of what went wrong. This cycle can repeat multiple times, each iteration further eroding your sense of self and reality.

Breaking the Cycle

Recognizing the cycle of abuse is the first step in breaking free from its grip. Here are strategies to help identify and escape this destructive pattern:

- **Awareness**: Educating yourself about narcissistic abuse and its cyclical nature is critical. Understanding that the idealization phase is a manipulation tactic, not a genuine expression of affection, can help you detach emotionally from the narcissist.

- **Support**: Building a support network of friends, family, or professionals who understand narcissistic abuse can provide the validation and encouragement needed to break free. Online and in-person support groups can be invaluable resources for sharing experiences and strategies.

- **Boundaries**: Establishing and maintaining firm personal boundaries is essential. This may include limiting contact with the narcissist, refusing to respond to attempts at manipulation, or ending the relationship entirely.

- **Self-Care**: Prioritizing your mental, emotional, and physical well-being can help rebuild the self-esteem and resilience eroded by the cycle of abuse. Activities that foster self-compassion, such as therapy, journaling, or meditation, can be particularly beneficial.

Survivor Stories

Hearing from those who have successfully navigated their way out of narcissistic abuse can offer hope and practical insights. One survivor, Alex, recounts how recognizing the cycle was a turning point: "It was like a lightbulb went off when I learned about the cycle of abuse. I could see the pattern in my relationship and, for the first time, understood it wasn't my fault." Alex emphasized the role of a support group in providing the strength to leave the relationship and the importance of therapy in healing from the trauma.

Another survivor, Jordan, shared the significance of boundaries: "Setting firm boundaries was hard, especially during the idealization phases when everything seemed perfect again. But reminding myself of the cycle and sticking to my boundaries saved me from falling back into the trap."

These stories underscore the importance of awareness, support, boundaries, and self-care in breaking free from the cycle of narcissistic abuse. They also highlight the strength and resilience of survivors, serving as a testament to the possibility of recovery and renewal.

Chapter 4: The Mask of Narcissism

Public vs. Private Self

Narcissists often exhibit a striking duality in their personalities, presenting a charming, likable facade to the outside world while revealing a more manipulative, often cruel nature in private settings. This dichotomy not only serves their need for admiration and validation from a wider audience but also enables them to control and dominate their closest relationships without external interference.

Dual Personalities

The disparity between how narcissists behave in public versus private can be jarring. In social situations, they typically exude charm and charisma, often becoming the life of the party or the person everyone wants to know. This public persona, often characterized by grandiose stories of success or adventure, displays of generosity, and a veneer of sensitivity and empathy, is meticulously crafted to attract admiration. In contrast, this facade falls away within the confines of personal relationships, revealing a propensity for emotional manipulation, criticism, and sometimes outright hostility towards those closest to them.

Maintaining the Facade

The effort narcissists put into maintaining their public image is no small feat. They are acutely aware of the perception others have of them and go to great lengths to protect and enhance their image. This can include exaggerating achievements, fabricating stories to garner sympathy or admiration, and strategically forming alliances with individuals who can elevate their social standing. The motivation behind this relentless pursuit of admiration is multifaceted, rooted in a deep-seated insecurity and an insatiable need for validation that their private self could never fulfill.

For narcissists, the public image is a shield, a carefully constructed barrier that prevents the outside world from seeing their true nature. This facade allows them to manipulate the narrative of who they are and serves as a defense mechanism against any form of criticism or accountability for their actions.

Impact on You

For those entangled in a close relationship with a narcissist, the contrast between the public charm and private torment can be a source of deep confusion and dissonance. You often find yourself questioning your perception of the narcissist, wondering if the loving, attentive partner or friend you occasionally see in private moments is the real person, overshadowed by stress or external pressures. This hope that the narcissist's better self will prevail can keep you trapped in a cycle of abuse, continually excusing unacceptable behavior in anticipation of a return to the idealization phase.

The impact of this duality extends beyond confusion; it can erode your trust in your own judgment, isolate you from external support systems, and instill a sense of unworthiness and despair. The private cruelty juxtaposed with public adoration leaves you questioning your reality as the charming public persona the narcissist presents makes it difficult for others to believe your accounts of abuse.

Seeing Behind the Mask

Recognizing the discrepancies between a narcissist's public and private selves is a critical step in understanding the true nature of the relationship and beginning the journey toward healing. Here are some strategies for discerning the mask from the true face:

- **Consistency in Behavior**: Pay attention to consistent patterns of behavior rather than isolated incidents of kindness or cruelty. Narcissists' public actions are often performative, designed to elicit a specific reaction or perception from others, whereas their private behavior reveals their true priorities and values.

- **Reactions to Criticism**: Observe how they respond to criticism or perceived slights in different settings. In public, narcissists may maintain their composure or deflect with charm, but in private, they may react with disproportionate anger or punishment.

- **Listen to Your Intuition**: Trusting your instincts is often challenging after experiencing gaslighting, but often, your gut feelings can alert you to discrepancies in the narcissist's persona.

- **Seek External Perspectives**: Confiding in trusted friends or a therapist can provide an outside perspective on the narcissist's behavior. These individuals can offer validation of your experiences and help you distinguish between the narcissist's true self and the facade.

Understanding the mask of narcissism requires recognizing that the public charm is as much a part of the narcissist's manipulation tactics as the private cruelty. By identifying this duality, you can begin to detach your sense of reality and self-worth from the narcissist's influence, laying the groundwork for reclaiming your autonomy and beginning the healing process.

Chapter 5: Trauma Bonding

The Chains That Bind

The concept of trauma bonding illuminates one of the most perplexing aspects of abusive relationships: the strong, often inexplicable attachment formed between an abuser and their target, particularly in the context of narcissistic abuse. This bond, paradoxical in its nature, ties you to the abuser through a series of highs and lows that create a powerful emotional connection that is difficult to break.

Definition of Trauma Bonding

Trauma bonding occurs when cycles of abuse and periods of tenderness or remorse from the abuser lead to a strong emotional attachment from the target. This bond is reinforced by the cyclical nature of narcissistic abuse, where moments of affection and promises of change are interspersed with episodes of manipulation, degradation, and cruelty. The intermittent kindness acts as a reward in a sea of punishment, leaving you clinging to hope for the return of the person you initially fell for.

Psychological Mechanics

The psychological underpinnings of trauma bonding are rooted in the concept of intermittent reinforcement. In this pattern, rewards (in this case, moments of kindness or affection) are given sporadically and unpredictably amidst a larger context of abusive behavior. This unpredictable pattern creates a pathological attachment as you become conditioned to endure the abuse with the hope of experiencing rewarding moments of kindness. This mechanism is akin to gambling; the uncertainty of the reward increases its perceived value, compelling you to stay in the relationship despite the abuse.

The manipulation of fear and love within these relationships further complicates your emotions. The abuser instills fear through their abusive actions, only to intermittently soothe this fear with expressions of love or remorse. This creates a confusing duality where you associate relief from fear and emotional pain with the very presence of the abuser.

Recognizing the Signs

Identifying trauma bonding within yourself can be challenging, as the bond itself clouds judgment and perpetuates denial. However, some signs may indicate the presence of a trauma bond:

- **Rationalizing Abuse**: Finding excuses for the abuser's behavior or downplaying the abuse.

- **Difficulty Leaving**: Feeling unable to leave the relationship despite recognizing its harmful nature.

- **Withdrawal from Support Systems**: Isolating from friends and family who express concern about the relationship.

- **Intense Fear of Abandonment**: Experiencing overwhelming fear at the thought of losing the relationship, regardless of how abusive it may be.

- **Fantasizing About the Abuser Changing**: Clinging to the hope that the abuser will return to the idealized version of themselves presented during the idealization phase.

Acknowledging these signs within yourself can be the first step toward breaking free from the chains of a trauma bond.

Breaking Free

Severing a trauma bond necessitates a multi-faceted approach, focusing on support, therapy, and self-care to navigate the complex emotions and withdrawal symptoms that accompany the separation from an abuser.

- **Seek Professional Help**: Engaging with a therapist who understands the dynamics of narcissistic abuse and trauma bonding can provide the guidance and support necessary to untangle the emotional web that binds you to the abuser.

- **Rebuild Support Networks**: Reconnecting with friends and family or seeking out support groups for survivors of narcissistic abuse can offer the external validation and encouragement you need to reinforce the decision to leave the abusive relationship.

- **Educate Yourself**: Understanding the mechanisms of trauma bonding and narcissistic abuse empowers you to recognize manipulation tactics and reinforce your resolve to break free.

- **Self-Care Practices**: Focusing on your well-being through activities that promote physical, emotional, and mental health can help rebuild the self-esteem and independence eroded by the abusive relationship. Activities might include exercise, meditation, journaling, or engaging in hobbies and interests that were neglected during the relationship.

- **Create a Safety Plan**: For those in situations where leaving may provoke retaliation from the abuser, developing a safety plan that addresses immediate physical, emotional, and financial safety is crucial. This plan may involve securing a place to stay, setting aside emergency funds, and informing trusted individuals about the situation.

Breaking free from a trauma bond is undeniably challenging, marked by moments of doubt, longing, and emotional turmoil. However, it is a critical step toward healing and reclaiming autonomy over your life. The path to recovery is personal and non-

linear, filled with setbacks and breakthroughs. Engaging in therapeutic work, leaning on supportive relationships, and prioritizing
self-care can gradually loosen the grip of the trauma bond, paving
the way for the journey to healing and self-discovery.

Chapter 6:
Psychological Impact
PTSD and C-PTSD in the Aftermath

Living through narcissistic abuse, individuals often emerge carrying invisible wounds that profoundly affect their mental health. Among these, Post-Traumatic Stress Disorder (PTSD) and Complex PTSD (C-PTSD) are significant conditions that can develop, altering the very fabric of one's emotional and psychological well-being. Make no mistake: these conditions actually change the chemical composition in the brain. While both stem from traumatic experiences, understanding their distinctions is crucial for identifying symptoms and seeking appropriate treatment.

PTSD typically results from a single, identifiable traumatic event, leaving individuals haunted by vivid memories, nightmares, and severe anxiety that disrupt daily life. Conversely, C-PTSD arises from prolonged exposure to trauma, particularly in environments where escape seems impossible—much like enduring narcissistic abuse. The complexity of C-PTSD encompasses not only the symptoms of PTSD but also deeper issues related to self-worth, emotional regulation, and relational challenges.

Recognizing the signs of these conditions marks the first step towards healing. Common symptoms include:

- **Flashbacks and Nightmares**: Reliving the trauma through vivid, intrusive memories or dreams.

- **Avoidance**: Steering clear of people, places, or situations that remind one of the trauma, often leading to isolation.

- **Negative Changes in Thoughts and Mood**: Feelings of hopelessness, memory problems, negative thoughts about yourself or others, and a pervasive sense of emotional numbness.

- **Heightened Arousal and Reactivity:** Being easily startled, feeling tense, having difficulty sleeping, and experiencing angry outbursts.

For those navigating the aftermath of narcissistic abuse, these symptoms can be both bewildering and overwhelming, stirring confusion about their origins and how to address them.

Healing from PTSD and C-PTSD is a path marked by patience and persistence. Evidence-based treatments have shown significant promise in aiding recovery:

- **Trauma-Focused Cognitive Behavioral Therapy (TF-CBT)**: This therapy aims to reframe negative thoughts about the trauma, incorporating coping strategies to manage distressing symptoms.

- **Eye Movement Desensitization and Reprocessing (EMDR)**: EMDR helps process and integrate traumatic memories, reducing their emotional impact.

- **Medication**: PTSD and C-PTSD alter the chemicals and neurotransmitters in the brain. While not a standalone solution, medications can reinstate and maintain balance in these systems, enabling rational thought and creating a more stable foundation for healing and moving forward.

- **Support Groups**: Connecting with others who have similar experiences fosters a sense of community and understanding, breaking the isolation that often accompanies these conditions.

Healing is a deeply personal journey, and what works for one individual may not suit another. Exploring various therapeutic approaches, sometimes in combination, can uncover the most effective path to recovery.

Among those who have traversed the rocky terrain of narcissistic abuse and emerged on the other side, their stories of healing illuminate the possibility of reclaiming life and finding peace. For instance, a person who endured years of narcissistic manipulation found solace and strength in EMDR therapy, which helped them process their trauma without being consumed by it. Another individual credits support groups as the turning point in their recovery, offering a safe space to share their experiences and learn from others who understand the depth of their pain. While still another found strength in their faith that enabled them to see their true value in this world and empowered them to move forward with courage.

These personal accounts, each unique in their challenges and triumphs, underscore the resilience of the human spirit. They remind us that while the scars of narcissistic abuse are real, so too is the capacity for healing and renewal.

Chapter 7: The Empath's Dilemma

Attraction and Vulnerability

In the intricate dance of human relationships, the dynamic between empaths and narcissists stands out with its profound complexity. Empaths are deeply attuned to the emotions and needs of others, often feeling them as intensely as their own. This inherent sensitivity equips them with a remarkable capacity for compassion, understanding, and nurturing—the very traits that can attract narcissists, as sharks are attracted to the smell of blood.

Empathy vs. Narcissism

The contrast between empaths and narcissists is stark. Empaths thrive on genuine connections, deriving satisfaction from the well-being of those around them. They listen attentively, offer support without hesitation, and highly value emotional authenticity. Narcissists, in contrast, seek relationships that serve their ego and need for admiration, viewing others primarily as sources of validation rather than as equals in a mutually respectful partnership. This fundamental mismatch in needs and intentions sets the stage for a precarious relationship dynamic, where the narcissist's manipulative tendencies can exploit the empath's generosity and compassion.

Vulnerability to Narcissistic Abuse

Empaths' openness and willingness to give often leave them vulnerable to narcissistic abuse. Their instinct to heal and comfort finds a seemingly perfect target in the narcissist, who expertly portrays themselves as needing and deserving of the empath's care. However, this dynamic can quickly become one-sided, with the empath pouring emotional energy into a bottomless pit of the narcissist's demands, often at the cost of their own well-being. The empath's desire to see the good in others and to focus on potential rather than present behavior can lead them to overlook red flags and boundaries, making them susceptible to being drawn into the narcissist's orbit.

Empaths might also misinterpret the intensity of the relationship with a narcissist as a deep, soulful connection, mistaking manipulation and control for passion and love. This misinterpretation can trap them in a cycle of trying to "fix" or "save" the narcissist, a futile endeavor that only leads to further emotional depletion.

Protecting Empathy

For empaths, safeguarding our empathetic nature while avoiding the pitfalls of narcissistic relationships involves conscious effort and self-awareness. Strategies include:

- **Boundaries**: It is crucial to learn to set and enforce healthy boundaries. We must recognize that saying "**No**" is both a right and a form of self-respect. It's about understanding where you end and another person begins, protecting your energy and emotional well-being.

- **Self-reflection**: Regular self-reflection helps us distinguish between our emotions and those we absorb from others. Practices like journaling and mindfulness can help develop this self-awareness, ensuring we remain centered on our own feelings and needs.

- **Selective Sharing**: We should be cautious about how much they share and with whom. By opening up gradually and observing how the other person responds to your vulnerability, you can better assess whether a relationship is balanced and healthy.

- **Education**: Understanding the traits of narcissistic personality disorder and recognizing the early signs of narcissistic behavior can empower you to steer clear of potentially harmful relationships. Knowledge about these dynamics can also help you extricate yourself from abusive situations more readily.

Empath Empowerment

Transitioning from vulnerability to empowerment involves a shift in perspective for empaths. You will start to view your sensitivity not as a weakness but as a source of strength. This reframing enables you to harness your empathetic nature for your benefit and the good of those who genuinely appreciate and reciprocate your compassion.

You possess an innate ability to read others and sense emotional undercurrents, which, when coupled with knowledge and boundaries, can become a powerful tool in identifying and resisting narcissistic abuse. You will learn to trust your intuition when it signals something is amiss and act on these insights by distancing yourself from toxic individuals.

Moreover, you can channel their nurturing energy toward mutually supportive and enriching relationships, investing in connections that honor empathy rather than exploit it. This will not only protect your well-being but also attract individuals who value and mirror your depth of care and understanding.

Fostering online or in-person communities based on empathy and mutual respect can offer solace and strength. These spaces offer validation and a reminder that the gift of empathy is not a burden but a beacon of hope and healing in a world that sorely needs it.

Through your journey of self-discovery and empowerment, you will emerge with a profound understanding of your worth and the transformative power of your empathy. You will learn that true strength lies in your ability to care deeply, to establish limits that honor your well-being, and to choose relationships that celebrate, not diminish, your inherent capacity for compassion. This realization marks a pivotal point in reclaiming your energy and shaping a life that reflects *your* values, one where empathy shines as a gift, illuminating the path forward.

Chapter 8: Narcissistic Supply and Demand

Feeding the Ego

The term "narcissistic supply" refers to the psychological concept where individuals with narcissistic tendencies seek constant validation, admiration, and attention to fuel their inflated self-esteem and ego. This supply acts as a drug, with narcissists craving it to maintain their sense of superiority and self-worth. Without it, they often feel empty, worthless, or depressed, leading them to seek out new sources of supply relentlessly.

The Concept of Narcissistic Supply

Understanding narcissistic supply requires recognizing its role as the lifeblood of individuals with narcissistic personality traits. It's what keeps their outward appearance of confidence and grandiosity inflated. The supply can come in various forms, but its essence lies in affirming the narcissist's perceived greatness and importance. It's not merely attention that they seek; it's a specific type of validation that mirrors their inflated, manufactured self-image back to them, reinforcing their exaggerated self-perceptions.

Sources of Supply

Narcissists find their supply in numerous places, drawing from both positive and negative interactions:

- **Adoration and Admiration**: The most straightforward source is outright adoration and admiration from others. Compliments, praise, and expressions of envy or desire all serve to inflate the narcissist's ego.

- **Accomplishments and Achievements**: Successes, whether in professional or personal arenas, offer a form of supply by validating the narcissist's belief in their superiority and exceptionalism.

- **Control and Power**: Exercising control over others, whether through manipulation, intimidation, or coercion, provides a potent form of supply. It reinforces their self-image as powerful and influential.

- **Fear and Subservience**: Inducing fear or subservience in others also serves as a supply. It reaffirms the narcissist's perception of themselves as an omnipotent figure worthy of deference.

The Role of the Target

Targets of narcissistic abuse unknowingly become a primary source of narcissistic supply. Through their reactions—pain, confusion, anger, or attempts to please—they validate the narcissist's sense of power and importance. This dynamic sets the stage for the cyclical nature of abuse, where the target's responses to manipulation and mistreatment feed directly into the narcissist's need for supply, encouraging further abusive behaviors.

In this context, targets often find themselves trapped in a paradoxical situation. Their natural responses to abuse, intended to mitigate conflict or seek reconciliation, inadvertently become the very fuel that sustains the cycle, making it exceedingly difficult to break free from the narcissist's grip.

Cutting Off the Supply

Halting the flow of narcissistic supply is a critical step for targets looking to escape the cycle of abuse. This process involves several key strategies:

- **Establishing Boundaries**: Clear, firm boundaries are vital. This might mean refusing to react to provocations, setting limits on communication, or, in some cases, ending the relationship entirely. Boundaries signal to the narcissist that their usual tactics no longer yield the desired supply.

- **Implementing No Contact**: Cutting off all forms of communication with the narcissist effectively starves them of supply. This approach can be challenging, especially if there are logistical ties like shared custody of children, but maintaining as much distance as possible is crucial for healing.

- **Reclaiming Personal Power**: You will reclaim your power by focusing on your own needs, desires, and well-being rather than the narcissist's demands. This shift reduces the emotional and psychological energy available to feed into the narcissist's supply, weakening the cycle of abuse.

- **Seeking Support**: Engaging with a support network or professional help can provide the strength and perspective needed to maintain these boundaries and resist the temptation to respond to the narcissist's attempts to regain supply.

By cutting off the supply, you not only protect yourself from further abuse but also disrupt the dynamic that empowers the narcissist, paving the way for a life free from the cycle of narcissistic abuse. This process is not instantaneous and involves navigating complex emotions and challenges. However, with persistence, support, and a focus on personal healing, it is possible to move beyond the reach of the narcissist's influence.

In this pursuit, remember that the objective is not to punish the narcissist by withholding supply but to prioritize and safeguard your own well-being. The journey away from being a source of narcissistic supply and towards becoming an advocate for your happiness and health marks a pivotal shift in reclaiming the narrative of your life from the shadow of narcissistic abuse.

Part 2: Initiating the Detachment Process

Stepping away from the shadow of a narcissist requires more than just physical distance; it demands an internal shift, a reclamation of the self that was lost in the whirlwind of manipulation and control. This chapter lays the groundwork for that pivotal move, guiding you through the initial, often daunting phases of separating from a narcissist. Here, the focus is not just on leaving the narcissist; it is about embarking on a path that leads back to *yourself*.

> *"Sometimes walking away is the only option. Not because you want to make someone miss you, or realize they took you for granted, but because you finally respect yourself enough to say, 'I deserve better.'"*
>
> Charlotte Freeman

Chapter 1: The Decision to Leave

Overcoming Fear and Doubt

Acknowledging the Need to Leave

Realizing the detrimental impact a relationship has on your mental and emotional health marks a critical turning point. It is a moment of clarity, often arriving after months or years of confusion and suffering. Recognizing the toxic nature of the relationship is the first vital step toward detachment. It's not about assigning blame but understanding that the dynamic you are entrenched in is harmful and unsustainable.

Overcoming Emotional Hurdles

The thought of leaving can trigger a storm of emotions—fear, guilt, and doubt chief among them. Each emotion acts as a barrier, complicating the decision to step away.

- **Fear:** It's natural to fear the unknown. Life after leaving might seem daunting, especially if the narcissist has become a central figure in your world. Counteract this fear by focusing on the reasons for leaving. Visualize the peace and autonomy that await you on the other side of this decision.

- **Guilt**: Guilt often arises from the belief that you're abandoning someone in need. Remember, a narcissistic individual's needs are bottomless. Your responsibility is to your well-being, not to fix or save another at your expense.

- **Doubt**: Doubt creeps in, whispering that maybe things aren't as bad as they seem or that leaving is an overreaction. Reinforce your resolve by journaling about the relationship's impact on your life and talking to trusted individuals who have witnessed its effects on you.

Seeking Support

A robust support network is invaluable in this phase. Friends, family, and professionals can provide the strength and validation necessary to move forward. Here's how to leverage this support:

- **Friends and Family**: Turn to those who have your best interests at heart. Be open about your decision and the support you need, whether it's a listening ear or a place to stay temporarily.

- **Professionals**: Therapists or counselors specializing in narcissistic abuse can offer insights and coping strategies specific to your situation. Their objective perspective can be a grounding force amid emotional turmoil.

Planning Your Exit

Exiting from a narcissistic relationship requires careful planning, especially if cohabitation or financial entanglement is involved. Consider the following steps:

- **Financial Preparation**: Begin by securing your financial independence. Open a bank account in your name, redirect your paycheck, and set aside emergency funds.

- **Housing Arrangements**: If you live with the narcissist, research your housing options. Can you stay with friends or family temporarily? Are there affordable rentals in your area? There may also be resources available from local domestic violence agencies. Make arrangements discreetly to avoid tipping off the narcissist before you're ready to leave.

- **Legal Considerations**: If marriage or custody issues are involved, consult with a lawyer familiar with narcissistic abuse. They can guide you through the legal intricacies and help you prepare for potential challenges from the narcissist.

- **Document Abuse**: Keep a record of instances of abuse, including dates, details, and any evidence like texts or emails. This documentation can be crucial for legal proceedings and for reinforcing your reasons for leaving.

Visual Aid: Checklist for Planning Your Exit

To assist in this crucial step, consider creating a detailed checklist that covers all necessary preparations, including:

- Financial accounts and documents to secure

- Personal items to collect

- Legal documents to gather

- Support contacts to reach out to

- Safe places to stay

This checklist serves as a tangible plan that you can refer to, ensuring that no critical steps are overlooked in the process of detaching from a narcissistic relationship. It's a roadmap that leads away from abuse and towards a future of autonomy and peace.

In engaging with this chapter, remember that the decision to leave is profoundly personal. It is a step taken not out of malice or revenge but from a place of self-respect and a desire for a healthier, happier life. While the path ahead may be fraught with challenges, it is also lined with opportunities for growth, healing, and rediscovery.

Chapter 2: No Contact

Drawing the Line in the Sand

In the aftermath of deciding to leave a narcissistic relationship, severing all forms of communication stands as a formidable yet critical step towards healing. This section delves into the intricacies of implementing the no-contact rule, navigating its challenges, and embracing the solitude it brings as a space for recovery.

The No-Contact Rule: A Definition

The no-contact rule is an unequivocal boundary setting, a clear-cut from all forms of communication with the narcissist. It's not merely about avoiding in-person encounters; it extends to phone calls, texts, emails, and social media interactions. Why is this so vital? Engaging with a narcissist, even minimally, can drag you back into the cycle of abuse, hindering your healing process. No contact is about reclaiming your mental and emotional space, allowing you to focus on your recovery without interference.

Steps to Implement No Contact

Executing a no-contact strategy requires meticulous planning, especially when entanglements like shared responsibilities or assets exist. Here's how to approach this:

- **Digital Detachment**: Block the narcissist on all social media platforms and any communication apps. Change your phone number if necessary. The goal is to eliminate any digital pathway they might use to reach you.

- **Shared Responsibilities**: For those with children or business ties, maintaining complete no contact might be unrealistic. In such cases, limit communication to written forms like emails or texts, strictly about the shared responsibility. Consider using third-party communication services designed for separated parents, which can also document interactions for legal purposes.

- **Inform Your Circle**: Let close friends, family, and colleagues know about your decision to go no contact, requesting their support in not relaying messages from the narcissist. This step is crucial in closing any loopholes the narcissist might exploit to reach you.

- **Prepare Mentally**: Visualize scenarios where the narcissist might attempt to breach your no-contact rule. Planning your response can help you stick to your decision when emotions run high.

Navigating Challenges and Temptations

Staying steadfast in your no-contact decision will test your resolve. Here are common hurdles and strategies to overcome them:

- **Urges to Reach Out**: Moments of loneliness or nostalgia might tempt you to re-establish contact. Counteract this by reminding yourself of the reasons you chose to leave. Keep a journal where you've detailed the abuse and refer to it during weak moments.

- **The Narcissist's Attempts to Reconnect**: Narcissists often try to re-initiate contact, especially if they sense they're losing control. They might use guilt, anger, or feigned concern to get a response. Stay firm in your resolve by not engaging.

- **Mutual Acquaintances:** Sometimes, the narcissist will use mutual friends or family to relay messages or gather information about you. Make it clear to your acquaintances that you do not want to discuss the narcissist or receive messages from them.

The Onset of Healing

With the initiation of no contact, you set the stage for your recovery. While initially daunting, this solitude becomes a sanctuary for emotional and mental healing. Here is what to expect:

- **Emotional Rollercoaster**: The first weeks or months might bring a whirlwind of emotions—relief, sorrow, anger, and sometimes, doubt. Allow yourself to feel these emotions without judgment. It is part of the healing process.

- **Rediscovery of Self**: As the fog of narcissistic abuse begins to lift, you will start rediscovering your likes, dislikes, and interests that were suppressed in the relationship. Engage in activities that bring you joy and fulfillment.

- **Strengthening of Resolve**: Each day you maintain no contact, your resolve strengthens. You will find clarity and conviction in your decision as you notice improvements in your mental and emotional well-being.

- **Support System**: Leaning on your support system is crucial during this time. Whether friends, family or a support group for survivors of narcissistic abuse, surround yourself with people who understand and affirm your journey.

The initiation of no contact is not merely about cutting ties; it's about setting yourself free from the chains of manipulation and regaining control over your life. It marks the beginning of a journey where the focus shifts from surviving to thriving, from darkness to light, and from chaos to peace. This profound transition, facilitated by the silence that once seemed unbearable, becomes the foundation upon which you rebuild a life defined by self-respect, autonomy, and true happiness.

Chapter 3: Grey Rock Method

Becoming Uninteresting to the Narcissist

In the landscape of strategies to distance oneself from the grasp of a narcissist, the Grey Rock Method stands out for its subtlety and effectiveness. This approach is about making oneself as uninteresting as possible to the narcissist, turning into the emotional equivalent of a "grey rock": unremarkable, dull, and easily overlooked. The aim is to discourage the narcissist from pursuing interaction by offering no emotional response or engagement to feed their need for drama or attention.

For situations where cutting off all contact isn't viable, such as when children are involved or in professional settings where complete avoidance is impossible, the Grey Rock Method emerges as a practical alternative. It allows for necessary interactions while minimizing the emotional toll on the victim and reducing the narcissist's interest in them.

When No Contact Is Not Possible

Certain realities make the ideal of no contact unattainable. Co-parenting with a narcissist is a common scenario where some level of interaction is inevitable. In these instances, adopting a grey rock demeanor during exchanges about the children can keep interactions brief and emotionless, depriving the narcissist of the reaction they seek. Similarly, in a professional setting, where resigning isn't an option or might not be desired, this method helps maintain a safe emotional distance.

Dos and Don'ts

Successfully implementing the Grey Rock Method requires a careful balance. Here are some guidelines to navigate this approach effectively:

- **Do**:

    - **Keep conversations short and factual**. Stick to necessary information and avoid sharing personal feelings or opinions.

    - **Use monotone responses**. A lack of emotional inflection makes interactions less engaging for the narcissist.

    - **Focus on mundane topics**. Discussing neutral subjects like the weather can make interactions less appealing.

- **Maintain a calm demeanor**. Even if the narcissist tries to provoke a reaction, staying calm and composed can discourage further attempts.

- **Don't**:

  - **Engage in conflict**. Arguing or trying to defend yourself gives the narcissist the emotional response they crave.

  - **Share personal information or feelings**. This can provide ammunition for the narcissist to manipulate or hurt you.

  - **React to provocations**. Showing hurt, frustration, or anger feeds into the cycle of abuse.

  - **Overdo it**. Being too obvious in your attempts to be uninteresting might prompt the narcissist to increase their efforts to elicit a reaction.

Protecting Your Emotional Well-being

While the Grey Rock Method can be an effective way to manage interactions with a narcissist, it is crucial to acknowledge the emotional strain this strategy may entail. Constantly suppressing your reactions and emotions, especially in the face of provocation, can be exhausting and, over time, might even feel dehumanizing. To mitigate these effects, consider the following:

- **External Support**: Rely on friends, family, or a therapist to provide a safe space where you can express the emotions and thoughts you are holding back in the presence of the narcissist. Sharing your experiences and feelings can help validate them, offering relief and perspective.

- **Emotional Outlets**: Engage in activities that allow for emotional release and self-expression. Creative pursuits like writing, painting, or playing music can be particularly therapeutic, offering an escape from the emotional monotony of the grey rock facade.

- **Self-Care Practices**: Incorporate regular self-care routines that focus on emotional and physical well-being. Activities like yoga, meditation, or even simple walks in nature can help counterbalance the emotional strain of interactions with the narcissist.

- **Boundaries**: Even as you employ the Grey Rock Method, continue to reinforce personal boundaries. Decide in advance how much time you will allot for interactions with the narcissist and what topics are off-limits, ensuring that you retain control over your engagement level.

Approached with mindfulness, the Grey Rock Method can serve as a valuable tool in the difficult task of navigating life with a narcissist when no contact is not an option. By maintaining emotional neutrality and focusing on your well-being outside these interactions, you can minimize the impact of the narcissist on your life while safeguarding your emotional health.

Chapter 4: Legal and Financial Preparation

Protecting Your Assets

Stepping away from a relationship with a narcissist involves more than emotional detachment; it also necessitates a strategic approach to legal and financial matters. This crucial phase is about safeguarding your future and ensuring you have the foundation you need to rebuild.

Navigating Legal Challenges

When extricating yourself from a narcissistic relationship, particularly those entangled with marriage or shared assets, the legal landscape can appear daunting. The key here is early preparation. Start by collecting all relevant legal documents—marriage certificates, property deeds, financial statements, and any prenuptial agreements. Understanding your legal standing and rights is paramount.

It is not uncommon for narcissists to use legal proceedings as a battleground for exerting control or seeking vengeance. Anticipate potential challenges such as disputes over property, custody battles, or even defamation attempts. Preparing for these scenarios involves a few critical steps:

- **Secure Legal Representation**: Engage a lawyer familiar with narcissistic behaviors and their impact on legal disputes. This expertise is crucial for navigating the complexities of your case and for strategizing against a narcissist's tactics.

- **Gather Evidence**: Document instances of abuse or manipulation that may be relevant to legal proceedings. This could include emails, texts, voicemails, or witness testimonies.

- **Understand Your Rights**: Educate yourself on your legal rights and the likely outcomes of your case. This knowledge arms you with realistic expectations and helps in decision-making.

Financial Independence

Achieving financial independence is a cornerstone of your detachment process. For many, financial entanglement serves as a significant barrier to leaving a narcissistic relationship. Begin with these steps to secure your financial independence:

- **Separate Finances**: Open personal bank accounts and reroute your income away from any joint accounts. This step is critical for establishing financial autonomy.

- **Build Credit**: If your credit history is intertwined with the narcissist's or if you lack a credit history of your own, start building or improving your credit. Secure a credit card in your name and manage it responsibly to establish a good credit score.

- **Create a Budget:** Develop a budget that reflects your new financial reality. Prioritize essential expenses and savings for future security.

- **Understand Shared Debts**: Get a clear picture of any shared debts and understand your responsibilities. Consult with a financial advisor or lawyer to explore options for managing or negotiating these debts.

Documentation and Evidence

In both legal and financial matters, documentation is your ally. Keeping thorough records supports your case in legal proceedings and aids in disentangling your finances. Here's how to approach this:

- **Log Communications**: Keep a log of all interactions with the narcissist, especially those that could be relevant in court or financial disputes.

- **Save Financial Records:** Collect statements, bills, receipts, and any documents related to shared assets or debts. These records are crucial for proving ownership, contributions to shared assets, or discrepancies in financial reporting.

- **Photograph Property**: Take photographs of physical assets, especially those of significant value. This visual evidence can be helpful in property disputes.

Seeking Professional Help

The complexity of leaving a narcissistic relationship often requires guidance from professionals who understand the unique challenges involved. Below are examples of who might be on your team:

- **Lawyer**: As mentioned, a lawyer skilled in dealing with high-conflict divorces or separations can be invaluable. They can provide legal advice tailored to your situation, helping you navigate the challenges of litigation with a narcissist.

- **Financial Advisor**: A financial advisor can help you plan for your future, offering advice on budgeting, investments, and managing any shared debts. They can also guide you in securing your financial independence.

- **Therapist**: A therapist, especially one with experience in narcissistic abuse, can offer support and strategies for coping with the emotional stress of legal and financial battles.

Preparing for the legal and financial aspects of leaving a narcissistic relationship is about more than just gathering documents or securing assets; it's about laying the groundwork for a future where you are in control. This preparation not only equips you to face the challenges ahead but also serves as a crucial step in reclaiming your autonomy and setting the stage for a new chapter in your life.

Chapter 5: Creating a Support Network

Finding Allies

A network of supportive relationships offers a sanctuary of understanding, compassion, and practical help during times of significant change. This network becomes your sounding board, offering perspectives that ground you and encouragement that fuels your resolve to move forward.

The Role of a Support Network

A well-knit support network serves multiple roles in your life, especially when distancing yourself from a toxic relationship. It provides:

- **Emotional Comfort**: Friends, family, or group members ready to listen can offer comfort through empathy and shared experiences.

- **Practical Assistance**: From helping you find new accommodation to offering legal advice, your network can provide practical assistance in various forms.

- **Validation of Your Experience**: Having your feelings and experiences validated by others is crucial in reaffirming your reality, especially after being subjected to gaslighting or manipulation.

Building Your Network

Cultivating a robust support network requires intention and effort. Here are steps to guide you in building or strengthening your circle of allies:

- **Reconnect with Estranged Contacts**: Reach out to old friends or family members you've lost touch with due to the relationship. Honesty about your situation can reopen doors and rekindle these relationships.

- **Explore Support Groups:** Many find solace and strength in groups comprised of individuals who have faced similar challenges. Whether it is through local community centers or online platforms, these groups offer a space for shared healing.

- **Volunteer or Join Clubs**: Engaging in volunteer work or joining clubs that align with your interests can introduce you to like-minded individuals who might become part of your support network.

Online and Community Resources

The digital age brings a wealth of resources to your fingertips, offering support and information that can be crucial in your journey. Consider exploring:

- **Online Forums**: Platforms like Reddit and other specialized forums provide anonymous spaces where you can share your story, seek advice, and support others in similar situations.

- **Social Media Groups**: Facebook and other social media platforms host numerous groups dedicated to healing from narcissistic abuse. These can be valuable resources for advice, encouragement, and forming new friendships.

- **Advocacy Organizations**: Organizations focused on domestic abuse and mental health often have resources for those leaving toxic relationships, including hotlines, counseling services, and legal aid.

Setting Boundaries with Supporters

While building a network of support, maintaining your autonomy is vital. Setting boundaries ensures that your journey towards healing remains yours. Here is how to approach boundary setting:

- **Communicate Your Needs**: Be clear about what kind of support you are seeking, whether a listening ear, advice, or practical help. Let your supporters know how best they can assist you.

- **Limit Over-Reliance**: Relying too heavily on one person or group can strain relationships and hinder your growth. Spread your reliance evenly and remember the importance of self-reliance.

- **Privacy Settings**: Share only what you are comfortable with. Keeping certain aspects of your journey private, even from close supporters, is okay.

- **Respect Others' Boundaries**: Just as you set your own boundaries, be mindful and respectful of the limits set by your supporters. Mutual respect fortifies these relationships, making them more enduring and meaningful.

Building and nurturing a support network is an active process that evolves along with your needs and circumstances. As you move forward, this network becomes a cornerstone of your resilience, offering a blend of empathy, practical aid, and validation that reinforces your strength and independence. It's a reminder that while the path may be yours to walk, you do not have to walk it alone.

Chapter 6: Self-Care Strategies

Building Resilience for the Journey Ahead

Self-care emerges as a pivotal component in the narrative of healing from the scars left by narcissistic abuse. It stands as a testament to the resilience of the human spirit, a beacon that lights the path to recovery. The essence of self-care lies in actions and practices that nurture your physical, emotional, and mental health, fostering a sense of empowerment and well-being.

Physical Self-Care

The link between body and mind is undeniable, making physical self-care a critical aspect of your healing process. Here are practices that can significantly impact your mental health:

- **Regular Exercise**: Physical activity releases endorphins, the body's natural mood elevators. Activities like walking, yoga, or swimming can reduce stress levels, improve sleep, and enhance overall well-being.

- **Balanced Nutrition**: Nourishing your body with a balanced diet supports brain function and emotional stability. Incorporate a variety of fruits, vegetables, whole grains, and lean proteins into your meals to fuel your body and mind.

- **Restorative Sleep**: Prioritizing sleep is crucial for emotional resilience. Establish a calming nighttime routine and aim for 7-9 hours of sleep to help your body and mind recover from daily stresses.

Emotional Self-Care

Tending to your emotional health is equally essential, providing the tools to process and move through the complex emotions tied to leaving a narcissistic relationship:

- **Journaling**: Writing offers a private, reflective space to express feelings, fears, and hopes. It can clarify thoughts and emotions, revealing patterns and progress over time.

- **Therapy**: Engaging with a therapist who understands the dynamics of narcissistic abuse can offer profound insights and coping mechanisms. Therapy provides a supportive environment to explore your feelings and develop strategies for emotional regulation.

- **Mindfulness and Meditation**: These practices anchor you in the present moment, reducing anxiety and enhancing inner peace. Even a few minutes each day can make a significant difference in your emotional landscape.

Cultivating a Self-Care Routine

A sustainable self-care routine is not a luxury but a necessity on the road to recovery. Here's how to integrate self-care into your daily life:

- **Set Realistic Goals**: Start with small, achievable self-care actions. Whether it's a 10-minute walk, meditating for five minutes, or writing in a journal each night, these small steps accumulate to substantial benefits.

- **Schedule Self-Care Time**: Treat self-care as a non-negotiable part of your day. Blocking out time in your schedule ensures it becomes ingrained in your routine.

- **Diversify Your Practices**: Incorporate a mix of physical, emotional, and mental self-care activities. Variety keeps the routine engaging and addresses your needs on multiple levels.

- **Listen to Your Body and Mind**: Pay attention to what you need. Some days, you might crave the energy release of a workout; on others, you may need the quiet reflection of journaling. Flexibility in your self-care practice allows it to evolve with you.

Self-care is not a one-size-fits-all blueprint but a personal journey that respects your unique needs and circumstances. It is about making conscious choices each day that edge you closer to healing and empowerment. Through these practices, you rebuild your resilience and rediscover joy, strength, and the capacity for renewal.

By committing to these self-care strategies, you lay the foundations for a life characterized not by the shadows of the past but by the light of self-awareness, growth, and well-being. This commitment signals a profound act of self-love, a declaration that you are worthy of care and kindness.

As this chapter of your healing narrative draws to a close, remember that self-care is both a refuge and a springboard. It offers solace in moments of struggle and propels you toward a future where well-being, peace, and resilience are within your grasp. The practices and principles outlined here are not just stepping stones out of the aftermath of narcissistic abuse; they are building blocks for a life rich with self-compassion and empowerment.

In moving forward, let these strategies be your companions, reminding you of your strength, your worth, and your capacity to heal. As you continue to weave the tapestry of your recovery, know that each act of self-care is a stitch in a larger pattern of renewal and hope.

Part 3: Cultivating Inner Strength

Imagine standing in front of a mirror, seeing not just your reflection but glimpsing the depths of your resilience and warmth—a resilience that has been tested, a warmth that has been tried in the cold fires of narcissistic trauma. This image is not just a hopeful visualization; it is a potential reality as you learn to harness the power of self-compassion. This section peels back the layers of self-doubt and criticism to reveal the healing balm of self-compassion—your right and your resource in the aftermath of trauma.

> *"You have power over your mind - not outside events.*
> *Realize this, and you will find strength."*
> Marcus Aurelius, "Meditations"

Chapter 1: The Power of Self-Compassion

Healing from Within

Defining Self-Compassion

Self-compassion is treating yourself with the same kindness, concern, and support you offer a good friend when they are suffering. It is recognizing that being imperfect, making mistakes, and encountering life difficulties are inevitable aspects of being human. Kristen Neff, a leading self-compassion researcher, outlines three core components of self-compassion: self-kindness, common humanity, and mindfulness. It is crucial to understand that self-compassion is distinctly different from self-pity. While self-pity isolates and exaggerates personal suffering, self-compassion connects our experiences with those of others, fostering a sense of shared humanity and reducing isolation.

Practices to Cultivate Self-Compassion

Cultivating self-compassion can be a transformative practice, especially for those healing from narcissistic abuse. Here are some practical exercises:

- **Mindfulness Meditation**: Sit quietly, focus on your breath, and observe your thoughts and feelings without judgment. When you notice harsh self-criticism, gently redirect your focus to your breath and offer yourself words of kindness and understanding.

- **Self-Compassion Journal**: Self-compassion journaling can be a powerful tool for nurturing kindness and understanding towards oneself, especially during challenging times. Here are examples of self-compassion journal prompts to help cultivate a more compassionate relationship with yourself:

  - **Reflect on a recent challenge**: Write about a current or recent challenging situation. How did it make you feel? Show compassion to yourself by acknowledging these feelings without judgment.

  - **Write a letter to yourself**: Compose a letter to yourself from the perspective of a compassionate friend. What would this friend say about how you have been treating yourself?

  - **Identify your strengths**: What are three qualities you like about yourself? Describe a situation where these strengths helped you or could help you in the future.

- **Forgive yourself**: Think of a mistake you have been holding onto. Write about it and explore ways to forgive yourself. What have you learned from this experience?

- **Comfort your inner child**: Imagine you could speak to your younger self. What words of comfort, encouragement, or advice would you offer?

- **Gratitude for your body**: What are three things you appreciate about your body and its capabilities? Reflect on how your body supports you in daily life.

- **Set healthy boundaries**: Reflect on your current boundaries. Are there areas in your life where you need to establish or reinforce boundaries? How would setting these boundaries be an act of self-compassion?

- **Respond to your inner critic**: Write down a recent critical thought you had about yourself. Now, challenge this thought with three compassionate responses.

- **Celebrate a small win**: What is a victory, no matter how small, you have achieved recently but have not given yourself credit for? Celebrate this achievement and reflect on its importance.

- **Envision a compassionate day**: Imagine a day where you treat yourself with utmost compassion and kindness. What does this day look like? How do you speak to yourself, and what activities do you engage in?

These prompts are designed to help you explore your feelings, thoughts, and behaviors from a place of kindness and understanding, encouraging a gentler and more forgiving relationship with yourself.

Overcoming Self-Criticism

The inner critic can be a loud voice, especially after experiences of narcissistic abuse. Here are strategies to soften its harshness:

- **Identify and Name**: Recognize when your inner critic is speaking. Naming this voice can help you separate it from your true self.

- **Challenge and Replace**: Challenge the validity of the critic's messages. Ask yourself, "Is this really true?" Then, actively replace these messages with kinder, more compassionate responses.

- **Gratitude Journaling**: At the end of each day, write down three things you're grateful for about yourself. This practice can shift focus from self-criticism to self-appreciation.

The Impact on Healing

Self-compassion is not just a feel-good concept; it can significantly accelerate the healing process. It encourages a nurturing and forgiving relationship with yourself, providing a safe internal space to process trauma and rebuild self-worth. Studies have shown that self-compassion is linked to lower levels of anxiety and depression, making it a powerful tool in the recovery from narcissistic abuse, as well as building a foundation of kindness and understanding that will support you in all of your future endeavors, relationships, and challenges.

Chapter 2: Establishing New Relationships
Trust and Vulnerability

After weathering the storm of a narcissistic relationship, the thought of opening up to someone new can feel akin to standing at the edge of a precipice. The drop is daunting, and the fear of falling once more is palpable. Yet, there is beauty on the horizon in the possibility of connections rooted in trust, respect, and mutual support. Let's navigate the landscape of forming new bonds, contrasting these hopeful beginnings with the shadows of the past.

Foundations of Healthy Relationships

The cornerstone of any enriching relationship is a solid foundation built on trust, respect, and mutual support. These elements stand in stark contrast to the instability characterizing interactions with a narcissist.

- **Trust** blooms in an environment where actions and words align, where promises are kept, and where vulnerabilities are handled with care. It's the antithesis of the unpredictability and betrayal experienced previously.

- **Respect** involves honoring each other's boundaries, valuing opinions, and celebrating differences. It's a refreshing departure from the disregard and devaluation endured.

- **Mutual Support** means being each other's cheerleader, offering a listening ear without judgment, and celebrating each other's successes. This reciprocity was often missing, as past dynamics were skewed towards the narcissist's needs.

Vulnerability as Strength

Vulnerability, the act of opening your heart despite the risk of hurt, is a testament to strength, not weakness. It is the bridge to genuine connection, allowing for a deep relationship unattainable behind walls of self-protection. Here's how to safely explore vulnerability:

- **Go Slow**: Allow vulnerability to unfold gradually. Share small pieces of yourself at a time, gauging the other person's response and building trust step by step.

- **Choose Wisely**: Be selective about who you open up to. Look for signs of empathy, respect, and kindness in their interactions with you and others.

- **Self-Reflection**: Pay attention to how being vulnerable makes you feel. If it is reciprocated with care and understanding, that is a positive sign. If it leaves you feeling exposed or diminished, it may be time to reevaluate.

Red Flags and Boundaries

Armed with the wisdom of past experiences, you're better equipped to spot early warning signs and establish healthy boundaries in new relationships.

- **Red Flags** might include consistent lateness (disrespecting your time), talking over you (disregarding your voice), or pushing boundaries (testing your limits). Acknowledging these signs early offers the chance to address them or walk away before deep emotional investment.

- **Setting Boundaries** is crucial. Clearly communicate your limits and deal-breakers from the outset. Boundaries are not ultimatums; they are expressions of your values and your need to feel respected and secure.

Building Trust Gradually

Trust is not a commodity to be handed out freely but a treasure to be built over time. It is the culmination of consistent, reliable actions and open, honest communication. Here is how to nurture trust in new connections:

- **Actions Over Words**: Pay attention to behavior. Are they reliable? Do their actions match their promises? Consistency in small matters builds trust in larger ones.

- **Open Communication**: Cultivate an environment where thoughts and feelings can be shared openly without fear of ridicule or dismissal. Practice active listening, showing genuine interest in understanding their perspective.

- **Maintain Independence**: Keep your hobbies, friendships, and interests alive. A healthy relationship involves two whole individuals coming together, not losing oneself in the other. Independence fosters trust by reducing pressure and expectations on the relationship to fulfill all emotional needs.

In stepping out to form new bonds, armed with the insights from past wounds and the courage borne from healing, you craft a path illuminated by hope. It's a path where trust is earned, respect is mutual, and vulnerability is met with kindness. Here, in the garden of new beginnings, you plant the seeds of relationships that offer the nourishment of genuine connection, watched over by the vigilant eyes of hard-earned wisdom.

Chapter 3: Breaking the Cycle

Avoiding Future Narcissists

Opening yourself up to new relationships after experiencing narcissistic abuse can feel like walking through a minefield blindfolded. You might question your ability to distinguish between genuine affection and manipulative charm. Here, we explore strategies to navigate this landscape, armed with insight and a renewed sense of self-worth.

Patterns That Attract Narcissists

Narcissists are adept at identifying individuals who exhibit specific emotional or behavioral patterns, viewing these traits as avenues for manipulation. Reflecting on past relationships can reveal these patterns, allowing for critical adjustments:

- **People-Pleasing Tendencies**: Constantly putting others' needs before your own can attract narcissists who thrive on exploiting generosity.

- **Low Self-Esteem**: Doubting your worth makes you

more susceptible to the narcissist's initial charm and subsequent devaluation, as you may feel unworthy of better treatment.

- **Fear of Confrontation**: Avoiding conflict at all costs signals to a narcissist that boundaries can be easily crossed without consequences.

- **Dependency on External Validation**: Seeking approval from others to feel valued can be a beacon for narcissists who use affirmation as a control tactic.

Changing these patterns involves cultivating self-awareness, assertiveness, and a strong sense of self-worth that does not hinge on others' opinions or actions.

Strengthening Emotional Boundaries

Emotional boundaries are your defense against future manipulation. They signal what you are and aren't willing to tolerate, protecting your mental and emotional well-being. Strengthening these boundaries requires:

- **Self-Reflection**: Identify what you value in relationships and what behaviors you will not tolerate. This clarity is crucial for setting firm boundaries.

- **Communication**: Clearly articulate your boundaries to others. Effective communication involves being direct yet respectful.

- **Consistency**: Enforce your boundaries consistently. Narcissists test limits, so demonstrating that your boundaries are non-negotiable is critical to deterring manipulation.

- **Self-Respect**: Upholding your boundaries is a form of self-respect. It affirms your right to be treated with kindness and consideration.

Awareness of Narcissistic Traits

Recognizing the red flags of narcissistic behavior can help you steer clear of potential harm. Familiarity with these traits allows for early detection, which is critical for protecting yourself:

- **Charm Offensive**: An overwhelming display of charm and affection early on, often termed "love bombing," is a tactic to fast-track intimacy and lower defenses.

- **Gaslighting**: Twisting the truth to make you question your reality is a hallmark of narcissistic manipulation. Be wary of individuals who consistently dismiss your feelings or memories.

- **Lack of Empathy**: A noticeable disinterest in your feelings or an inability to genuinely empathize with others can indicate narcissistic tendencies.

- **Entitlement and Exploitation**: Watch for signs of entitlement or a tendency to exploit others for personal gain, often masked by charm or feigned innocence.

Educating yourself on these and other narcissistic behaviors provides a lens through which to evaluate new acquaintances, allowing you to act on early warning signs.

Empowerment Through Choice

Realizing you have the power to choose who you let into your life is profoundly liberating. This empowerment stems from a deep belief in your worth and the knowledge that you deserve respect and kindness. Here is how to harness this power:

- **Trust Your Intuition**: Pay attention to gut feelings about people. Both conscious and subconscious observations inform intuition and can guide you away from harmful relationships.

- **Know Your Worth**: Internalize the fact that you deserve healthy, supportive relationships. This self-belief acts as a filter, helping you to avoid individuals who do not respect your worth.

- **Practice Assertiveness**: Being assertive about your needs and boundaries is not selfish; it is a healthy practice that signals to others how you expect to be treated.

- **Embrace Being Alone**: Recognize that being alone is preferable to being in a relationship where you feel undervalued. This perspective helps you to make choices from a place of strength rather than fear of loneliness.

In navigating the world post-narcissistic abuse, armed with these strategies, you step into a realm where history doesn't dictate the future. Here, informed by the past but not anchored to it, you move forward with a clear vision of the relationships you deserve. It's a landscape where boundaries are respected, where your worth is acknowledged, and where manipulation finds no foothold.

Chapter 4: Empowerment Through Knowledge

Educating Yourself and Others

In the wake of experiencing narcissistic abuse, your understanding of relationships, self-worth, and emotional health undergoes a seismic shift. Though born from hardship, this transformation opens up an invaluable avenue of empowerment—knowledge. Gaining insights into narcissism, its impacts, and the broader spectrum of psychological health is not just about personal healing; it is about fostering resilience and extending a hand to those navigating similar struggles.

Continual Learning

The path to recovery introduces a landscape rich with learning opportunities. Engaging with a variety of resources on narcissism and psychological well-being does more than fill gaps in understanding—it equips you with tools to rebuild and fortify your emotional resilience. Here are some strategies for incorporating learning into your recovery process:

- **Read Widely**: From academic texts to memoirs of recovery, reading offers insights into narcissistic behavior patterns and coping strategies. It also provides solace in shared experiences.

- **Attend Workshops and Seminars**: Participating in educational events led by psychologists or experts in narcissistic abuse can deepen your understanding and introduce you to the latest research and therapeutic approaches.

- **Online Courses**: Many universities and mental health platforms offer online courses on psychology and mental health, providing flexibility to learn at your own pace.

This commitment to learning not only aids in your healing but also prepares you to support others on their journey, creating a ripple effect of awareness and understanding.

Sharing Knowledge

As you navigate your healing process, sharing your newfound knowledge and experiences becomes a powerful tool for healing. It is an act of generosity that can illuminate the path for others, offering guidance and hope. Here are a few ways to share your journey and insights:

- **Blogging or Vlogging**: Sharing your story through a blog or video blog can reach individuals worldwide, offering support and understanding to those who feel isolated in their experiences.

- **Support Groups**: Whether leading a group or simply participating, sharing your insights in these spaces can foster a sense of community and collective healing.

- **Social Media**: Various platforms can be used to share quotes, insights, and personal reflections, reaching out to a broad audience with messages of hope and empowerment.

By sharing your story, you not only validate your experiences but also contribute to a larger narrative of survival and resilience, offering a beacon of hope to those still finding their way through the darkness of narcissistic abuse.

Advocacy and Awareness

Transforming personal pain into advocacy and awareness elevates your journey from one of survival to one of purpose. Advocacy is a powerful conduit for change, challenging the stigma surrounding narcissistic abuse and fostering a societal shift towards recognition and support. Here are some avenues for advocacy:

- **Participate in Awareness Campaigns**: Joining or initiating campaigns during Mental Health Awareness Month or Domestic Violence Awareness Month can help bring attention to narcissistic abuse.

- **Educational Talks**: Offering to speak at schools, universities, or community centers about narcissistic abuse and mental health can educate the public and empower others to seek help.

- **Collaborate with Mental Health Organizations**: Partnering with organizations to create resources or support legislative changes can have a lasting impact on how society addresses narcissistic abuse.

This activism contributes to societal change and reinforces your healing, turning the scars of your past into the strengths of the present and future.

Resources and Support

The journey of healing and empowerment is sustained by a network of resources and support systems. Here is a carefully curated list to guide you further:

- **Books**:

  - "In Sheep's Clothing: Understanding and Dealing with Manipulative People" by George K. Simon offers insights into recognizing and handling manipulation.

  - "The Body Keeps the Score: Brain, Mind, and Body in the Healing of Trauma" by Bessel van der Kolk explores the impact of trauma on the body and pathways to healing.

- **Websites**:

  - The National Domestic Violence Hotline (thehotlin

e.org) provides support and resources for those experiencing abuse.

- Psychology Today (psychologytoday.com) offers articles on narcissism, recovery, and finding therapists.

- **Support Groups**:

  - After Narcissistic Abuse - There is Light, Life & Love (ANA-LLC) offers online forums and resources.

  - Meetup (meetup.com) often lists local support groups for survivors of narcissistic abuse.

- **Podcasts**:

  - "Healing from Narcissistic Abuse" by Kelli Tennant provides personal stories and interviews with experts on recovery.

  - "Understanding Today's Narcissist" by Christine Hammond offers insights into narcissistic behaviors and coping strategies.

Embracing this wealth of resources enriches your understanding and strengthens your network of support, weaving a tapestry of knowledge, resilience, and community that upholds you as you rebuild your life. Through learning, sharing, advocating, and connecting, you transform the narrative of narcissistic abuse from one of victimhood to one of victory, empowerment, and hope.

Chapter 5: Nurturing Empathy

For Yourself and Others

In the aftermath of navigating through the tumultuous waves of narcissistic abuse, the concept of empathy, both directed towards oneself and extended to others, becomes a beacon of light. Through this lens of understanding and shared feelings, you can start to rebuild the fractured pieces of your inner world and forge meaningful and enriching connections.

The Role of Empathy in Healing

Empathy, at its core, is about resonating with the emotions of another, feeling with them, and understanding their perspective. When directed inward, it becomes a soothing balm that acknowledges one's pain, validates experiences, and fosters a nurturing internal environment conducive to healing. Learning to meet your emotional states with gentleness and comprehension lays the groundwork for extending this compassionate understanding to others, paving the way for relationships characterized by depth and genuine connection.

Turning empathy outward becomes a bridge to others' experiences, allowing for a deep, non-judgmental understanding. This reciprocal exchange of empathy strengthens bonds and aids in the collective healing process, creating a supportive network where individuals can find solace and strength.

Empathy vs. Enabling

It is crucial, however, to distinguish between *empathy* and *enabling*, especially in the context of recovering from narcissistic abuse. *Empathy* involves understanding and sharing the feelings of another, offering support while mutually respecting boundaries, and encouraging growth. In contrast, *enabling* involves actions that prevent others from facing the consequences of their destructive behavior, often at the cost of the enabler's well-being.

For those who have experienced narcissistic abuse, the line between empathy and enabling can sometimes blur, as the desire to understand and help the abuser might lead to justifying their actions or taking responsibility for their behavior. Recognizing this distinction is vital; genuine empathy empowers both the giver and receiver, fostering accountability and growth while enabling perpetuates harmful patterns.

Practicing Empathetic Listening

One of the most powerful ways to cultivate empathy is through empathetic listening, a skill that enhances the quality of interactions and the depth of relationships. Here are techniques to practice empathetic listening:

- **Full Attention**: Give the speaker your undivided attention. This means setting aside distractions, making eye contact, and adopting open body language to convey your presence and interest.

- **Reflective Responses**: Reflect back what you have heard, both the content and the emotions. This could be as simple as saying, "It sounds like you're feeling overwhelmed by this situation."

- **Hold Space**: Allow the speaker to express themselves without rushing to offer advice or solutions. Sometimes, the most empathetic response is simply to be present and acknowledge their feelings.

- **Validate Emotions**: Acknowledge the speaker's emotions without judgment. Validation can be profoundly comforting and is a cornerstone of empathetic listening.

Protecting Empathic Qualities

For those with a natural inclination towards empathy, especially survivors of narcissistic abuse, safeguarding this trait is essential. While empathy is a strength, it can also make one susceptible to emotional exhaustion or being taken advantage of if not balanced with self-care and boundaries. Here are strategies to protect your empathic qualities:

- **Self-Care Rituals**: Incorporate self-care practices into your daily routine to recharge your emotional batteries.

Whether it is through meditation, nature walks, or creative outlets, find activities that replenish your energy.

- **Set Emotional Boundaries**: Learn to recognize when you are taking on too much of another's emotional burden. It is okay to step back and compassionately communicate your need for space.

- **Seek Reciprocity**: Cultivate relationships where empathy is a two-way street. Surround yourself with individuals who understand and reciprocate your emotional generosity.

- **Mindful Engagement**: Be conscious of how much emotional energy you invest in understanding and supporting others. Engage in a way that honors your well-being and respects your limits.

In nurturing empathy within yourself and in relationships with others, you not only foster a healing internal environment but also contribute to a culture of understanding, compassion, and mutual support. Empathy becomes the thread that weaves through the tapestry of human connection, highlighting the shared nature of our experiences and the universal desire for understanding and kindness. Through empathetic engagement with both ourselves and those around us, we not only heal but also illuminate the path for others, offering a testament to the transformative power of empathy in the journey of recovery and beyond.

Chapter 6: The Importance of Community

Finding Strength in Numbers

Discovering a group of individuals who appreciate the depth of your experiences can transform the path to healing from a solitary walk into a shared voyage of discovery and mutual support. This sense of belonging to a community, whether found in the physical world or through the vast networks online, brings myriad benefits that can significantly impact your recovery and growth.

Finding Your Tribe

The search for a community that resonates with your experiences and provides a platform for shared stories and mutual understanding is a crucial step towards healing. Such communities offer more than just support; they provide a sense of belonging, validation of your experiences, and the reassurance that you are not alone. This tribe, your chosen family, becomes a source of strength, encouraging you through moments of doubt and celebrating your victories, no matter how small they may seem.

Online and Offline Communities

Both physical gatherings and online platforms have unique roles in fostering connections and offering support. Physical groups, found in local support meet-ups or specialized therapy groups, provide a tangible sense of connection, offering the comfort of human presence and the warmth of face-to-face interaction. On the other hand, online communities, accessible through forums, social media groups, or dedicated apps, break geographical barriers, offering a 24/7 haven for those seeking advice, sharing victories, or simply needing a space where they can be heard and understood.

- **Physical Groups**: These offer a space where the nuances of non-verbal communication—gestures, expressions, and the physical presence of others—add depth to the exchange of support and understanding.

- **Online Platforms**: They provide anonymity and accessibility, making it easier for many to share intimately and receive support without the constraints of location or the anxiety of physical meetings.

Participating in Community Healing

Engaging in community activities, such as workshops, group therapy sessions, or advocacy events, enriches the healing process. These gatherings are not just about receiving support; they're about contributing to the collective healing journey. Participation can take many forms:

- **Sharing Personal Stories**: Your story, with its unique challenges and triumphs, can be a source of inspiration and hope for others.

- **Volunteering**: Offering your time and skills to organize community events or support group activities strengthens the community's fabric and reinforces your sense of purpose and belonging.

These actions of giving back not only aid in your own recovery but also contribute to the creation of a nurturing environment where healing is a shared goal.

Creating Safe Spaces

The essence of a healing community lies in its ability to provide a safe, respectful, and confidential space for all its members. Establishing such an environment requires a collective commitment to uphold principles that ensure everyone feels heard, respected, and valued. Here are key aspects to consider:

- **Respect for Diverse Experiences**: Acknowledge and honor the unique paths each member has walked. This diversity enriches the community, providing a wider lens through which healing can be understood and approached.

- **Confidentiality**: A shared agreement on confidentiality fosters trust, making the community a safe haven for personal sharing.

- **Inclusivity**: Cultivating an atmosphere where everyone, regardless of their background or stage in their recovery, feels welcome and included is vital. This inclusivity strengthens the community's bond and its capacity to support its members.

- **Boundaries**: Setting and respecting personal boundaries within the community ensures that interactions remain supportive and do not become overwhelming or intrusive.

In nurturing these principles, the community becomes a sanctuary where healing is nurtured, and resilience is built, not in isolation but in the company of those who understand and support your journey.

As this exploration of community's role in healing and empowerment concludes, remember that the strength found in numbers, shared experiences, and mutual support is a powerful force on the path to recovery. The connections you forge, the stories you share, and the support you give and receive become the threads that weave together a tapestry of resilience, understanding, and renewed hope.

In moving forward, let the community be your ally, a source of strength, and a reminder that even in the darkest moments, you are not alone. Together with shared purpose and collective strength, the journey towards healing and empowerment continues, each step supported by the understanding and encouragement of those who walk beside you.

Make a Difference With Your Review!

Help Others Towards the Light

You are making great progress on your journey through "The Narcissistic Trauma Survival Guide." By turning each page, you've taken powerful steps towards understanding, healing, and reclaiming your life from the impact of narcissistic abuse. With the knowledge and insights you've gained thus far, you are now equipped with many of the tools you will need to forge a path of recovery and empowerment.

But the journey doesn't stop with this book. There's a way you can extend your hand to others who are just beginning to navigate their way out of the shadows of confusion and pain: by sharing your thoughts and experiences about this guide.

Leaving your honest review on Amazon is a simple yet profound way to pass on the torch of hope and guidance. Your words can illuminate the path for others, showing them where to find the support and understanding they desperately seek. It's more than just sharing your opinion; it's about connecting with a community of survivors and empowering them to take their first steps toward healing.

How Your Review Makes a Difference:

- Guides Others to Healing: Your review can be the signpost that directs someone to the help they need at a critical moment in their journey.

- Spreads Awareness: By sharing your insights, you contribute to the broader conversation about narcissistic abuse, helping to break the silence and stigma.

- Fosters Community: Your words can remind others that they are not alone, building a sense of solidarity and support among survivors.

Ready to Share Your Voice?

Simply scan this code!

Your contribution is invaluable. By leaving your review, you're not only keeping the conversation about narcissistic abuse alive but also helping to ensure that this vital support continues to reach those in need.

Thank you for sharing your journey and helping pass on the knowledge and strength you've gained. Together, we can keep the light of healing and recovery burning, supporting each other and future readers every step of the way.

Part 4: Tools for Everyday Living

Life after narcissistic trauma is a bit like discovering a favorite book that had gotten wet while in storage; the essence of what you loved is still there, but now it is about gently unfolding the pages, drying them out, and making sense of the smudged ink. It is a process requiring patience, care, and the right tools. This section is dedicated to providing you with those tools, simple yet effective practices you can weave into the fabric of your daily routine to aid in emotional regulation, stress reduction, and overall mental clarity.

"I am not what happened to me, I am what I choose to become." -
Carl Jung

Chapter 1: Mindfulness and Meditation

Tools for Emotional Regulation

The concept of *mindfulness* might bring images of serene landscapes or monks in deep meditation. However, at its core, mindfulness is about being fully present in the moment, an invaluable skill for anyone, but especially for those healing from trauma. It is like learning to navigate the ocean's waves instead of being pulled under by the current.

Benefits of Mindfulness

Mindfulness and meditation have been shown to significantly reduce stress, manage anxiety, and improve overall mood. Think of your mind as a sky and your thoughts as clouds. Some days, the sky is clear; other days, it's overcast. Mindfulness teaches you to observe these clouds without getting caught in a storm, recognizing that, just like the weather, your thoughts and feelings are temporary and constantly changing. For survivors of narcissistic abuse, this practice can be a lifeline, offering a way to step back from overwhelming emotions and gain perspective.

Simple Practices to Start

Starting a mindfulness practice does not require special equipment, training, or hours of your day. Here are a few exercises to get you started:

- **Focused Breathing**: Sit quietly and turn your attention to your breath. Notice the sensation of air entering and leaving your body. When your mind wanders, gently bring your focus back to your breath. Just five minutes of this exercise can act as a reset button for your nervous system.

- **Mindful Walking**: Next time you're walking, pay attention to the sensation of your feet touching the ground, the rhythm of your steps, and the sounds around you. It is a simple way to bring mindfulness into movement, turning an everyday activity into a meditative practice.

Incorporating Mindfulness into Daily Life

Mindfulness can color even the most mundane tasks with a sense of presence and calm. Here are tips for making mindfulness a part of your day:

- **Mindful Eating**: Take the time to really taste your food, appreciating the flavors and textures. It is a simple way to turn a daily necessity into a moment of mindfulness.

- **Pause Between Tasks**: Before jumping from one task to the next, take a moment to breathe and center yourself. It is a way to reset and bring mindfulness to your work or chores.

Resources for Deepening Practice

For those looking to deepen their mindfulness and meditation practice, a wealth of resources is available at your fingertips:

- **Apps**: Apps like Headspace and Calm offer guided meditations, mindfulness exercises, and even sleep stories to help integrate mindfulness into your life with ease.

- **Books**: "Wherever You Go, There You Are" by Jon Kabat-Zinn and "The Miracle of Mindfulness" by Thich Nhat Hanh provide insightful introductions to mindfulness practice, breaking down the concepts in accessible terms.

- **Courses**: Websites like Coursera and Udemy offer courses on mindfulness and meditation, often led by leading experts in the field. These courses range from beginner to advanced levels, accommodating everyone's needs.

Mindfulness and meditation are not just practices but pathways, offering a route to navigate the complexities of healing with grace and awareness. They remind us that in the midst of chaos, a center of calm is available to us, a place where we can find clarity, peace, and a sense of groundedness. Whether through focused breathing, mindful walking, or integrating mindfulness into daily tasks, these practices offer a way to gently unfold the pages of our lives, smoothing out the wrinkles left by trauma and making sense of our stories in a way that feels whole again.

Chapter 2: Journaling for Clarity and Reflection

In the gentle quiet of the morning or the soft stillness of the evening, there's a power found in the simple act of putting pen to paper. This intensely personal yet universally understood power is the essence of journaling. For those navigating the aftermath of narcissistic abuse, journaling emerges not just as an act of self-expression but as a tool for healing, offering a canvas on which the tangled emotions and thoughts can be laid bare, examined, and understood.

Therapeutic Benefits of Journaling

Beyond mere documentation of events, journaling is a therapeutic practice that facilitates a deeper understanding of your emotions, aids in processing trauma, and tracks the journey of healing. It allows for a conversation with yourself, a dialogue where feelings are acknowledged without judgment. This process of reflection can illuminate patterns in thoughts and behavior, offering insights that might remain obscured in the whirlwind of daily life. Furthermore, journaling solidifies experiences, making it possible to witness your growth over time, a beacon of progress on the days when the path ahead seems shrouded in fog.

Prompts to Begin

As we have previously discussed in the chapter on Self-Compassion, starting can often be the most challenging part. While the journaling in that chapter was more specific in nature, your journal at this point will be all-encompassing of your healing journey. Here are prompts designed to guide you gently into the practice, focusing on healing from narcissistic abuse, self-discovery, and carving out a vision for a future untethered from the past:

- Write a letter to your past self, offering the compassion and understanding you needed during moments of deep struggle.

- Describe a situation where you felt disempowered. What would empowerment have looked like in that moment?

- Imagine a day free from the shadows of the past. What does it look like, feel like, sound like?

- Reflect on a lesson learned from a challenging experience. How has this lesson shaped your path forward?

These prompts serve only as starting points, invitations to explore your inner landscape at your own pace, in your own words.

Creative Journaling Techniques

For some, the blank page can seem daunting, a vast space demanding eloquence and clarity. If traditional journaling feels restrictive, consider these creative approaches that invite color, texture, and imagery into the process:

- **Collage Journaling**: This technique involves creating visual entries using magazine clippings, photos, fabric, and other materials. It is particularly powerful for expressing emotions that words can't capture.

- **Art Journaling**: Incorporate doodles, sketches, or watercolors into your journal. The combination of art and words offers a multidimensional approach to reflection and expression.

- **Bullet Journaling**: For those who find structure comforting, bullet journaling organizes thoughts, tasks, and reflections through lists, symbols, and short entries, making the practice both practical and therapeutic.

These techniques affirm that there is no "right" way to journal; the method that resonates with you will be most beneficial.

Maintaining Privacy

The sanctity of your journal is paramount. It is a space where vulnerability takes center stage, where the rawest parts of your experience are laid out in ink. The thought of these pages being seen by prying eyes can stifle honesty, turning what should be a sanctuary into another source of stress. Here are strategies to ensure your journal remains a private refuge:

- **Digital Journaling**: Apps and digital journals protected by passwords offer a secure alternative to physical notebooks. Many apps also provide features like prompts and mood tracking.

- **Discreet Storage**: If you prefer the tactile experience of writing in a notebook, consider keeping your journal in a locked drawer or box. It's a simple measure that can provide significant peace of mind.

- **Camouflaged Cover**: Sometimes, disguising your journal as a mundane book or notebook can deter curious glances, allowing it to blend seamlessly into your bookshelf or desk.

The essence of journaling in the context of healing from narcissistic abuse is found in the unfiltered exploration of your thoughts, emotions, and aspirations. Whether through written words, collages, or sketches, the act of journaling carves out a space for self-reflection, offering clarity and insight on the journey to rediscovery and healing. With each page turned, the smudges of past experiences become part of a larger narrative, where growth, resilience, and hope are interwoven through reflection. As you continue to fill the pages of your journal, remember that each word, each mark, is a step towards understanding, a step towards a future where the past no longer casts its shadow over your path.

Chapter 3: Creative Expression

Healing Through Art

In the quiet moments that follow the storm of leaving a narcissistic relationship, finding a mode of expression that transcends words becomes not just a want but a need. In its myriad forms, art offers this escape, a way to articulate the inarticulable, to process the complex web of emotions and experiences that language alone cannot capture. It is in the brush strokes, the molding of clay, the click of a camera, that many find their feelings validated, their voices heard, and their healing accelerated.

Art as Therapy

Engaging in art as a form of therapy allows for a direct, unfiltered expression of the self. It is a dialogue between creator and creation that often reveals the subconscious, bringing to light emotions and thoughts that might have been buried or unacknowledged. This process can be profoundly liberating, as it offers a tangible way to confront and work through the residue left by narcissistic abuse. The act of creating becomes an act of self-discovery and, ultimately, self-recovery. It is not about the aesthetic value of the outcome but the act of creation itself. In this space, every color, texture, and shape holds meaning, each a piece of the puzzle that composes your inner world.

Starting with Simple Projects

For those unsure where to begin, starting simple can demystify the process of creative expression. Here are a few suggestions that require minimal skills but offer maximum therapeutic benefit:

- **Coloring Books for Adults**: These provide structured designs that you can fill with colors of your choice. The repetitive motion of coloring can be meditative, offering a sense of calm and focus.

- **Clay Modeling**: A lump of clay can become a tool for expression, with the tactile experience of shaping and molding providing a direct, hands-on way to channel emotions.

- **Scrapbooking**: Combining photographs, ticket stubs, and other memorabilia into a scrapbook allows for a reflective journey through memories, capturing both the bitter and the sweet.

These activities highlight that the journey into art therapy does not require grand gestures or sophisticated skills; it starts with one simple step, one simple project, and grows from there.

Exploring Different Mediums

Diving deeper into the world of art uncovers a spectrum of mediums, each offering a unique way to convey emotions and experiences. Exploring these avenues can help you find the one that resonates most deeply with you:

- **Painting**: Whether watercolor, acrylic, or oils, painting offers a broad canvas to express emotions. The fluidity of the medium can mirror the complexity of feelings, providing a release for pent-up emotions.

- **Sculpture**: Working with materials like clay or wood, sculpture brings the therapeutic process into three dimensions, offering a tangible way to "shape" your experiences and emotions.

- **Digital Art**: For those more inclined towards technology, digital art offers endless possibilities for creation, with software allowing for experimentation without the need for physical materials.

Exploring these mediums is a journey in itself, where the destination is less about the artwork produced and more about the insights gained and the emotions processed along the way.

Art Communities

Finding others who share a passion for creative expression can amplify the benefits of art as therapy. These communities, whether found locally or online, offer a space to share your work, gain inspiration, and connect with others on a similar path. Here's how to find these communities:

- **Local Workshops and Classes**: Many community centers, colleges, and art studios offer classes that teach skills and foster camaraderie among participants.

- **Online Platforms**: Websites like DeviantArt, Instagram, and specific forums dedicated to art therapy provide global platforms to share your work, receive feedback, and connect with fellow artists and survivors.

- **Exhibitions and Art Shows**: Participating in or attending local art exhibitions can connect you with the local art scene, offering opportunities to meet artists and view art through the lens of shared experiences.

These communities, whether virtual or physical, underscore the universal language of art. They remind us that our experiences, while uniquely our own, share common threads with others. In this shared space, the act of creating becomes not just a personal journey of healing but a collective one, where each piece of art contributes to a larger narrative of resilience, understanding, and hope.

In this exploration of art as therapy, it becomes clear that the value lies not in the masterpiece created but in the process of creation itself. It's in this process that we find a way to voice the unvoiced, to make tangible the intangible, and to transform the pain of the past into the beauty of expression. As we navigate the path of healing from narcissistic abuse, art stands as a faithful companion, offering a means to explore, express, and eventually to heal.

Chapter 4: Physical Wellness

The Mind-Body Connection

The interplay between our physical health and mental well-being is a dance as old as time itself. This intricate ballet, where each influences the rhythm of the other, highlights the undeniable fact that to truly heal from the inside out, we must pay homage to both our mental and physical selves. This dual focus acts as a catalyst for holistic healing, especially vital for those mending from the scars of narcissistic abuse.

Understanding the Mind-Body Connection

The dialogue between mind and body is continuous, a constant back-and-forth that shapes your experience of health. When your mental health quivers under the weight of stress or trauma, your physical health often echoes this disturbance. Conversely, when your physical health is compromised, it's not uncommon to find your mental state wavering. Recognizing this connection is the first step in leveraging it to foster healing. By nurturing your physical health, you can create a ripple effect that soothes and strengthens your mental well-being, providing a solid foundation upon which to build your recovery.

Simple Exercises to Get Started

Incorporating exercise into your daily routine need not be a daunting task. Simple, low-impact activities can seamlessly blend into your life, offering a gentle nudge to both your physical and mental health:

- **Walking**: The simplicity of a walk, whether around the neighborhood or through a local park, offers a double-edged sword of physical exercise and mental relaxation. The rhythmic pace and exposure to nature can act as a meditative practice, clearing the mind and invigorating the body.

- **Yoga**: This ancient practice combines physical poses with breathing techniques, promoting flexibility, strength, and a sense of inner calm. Yoga sessions, even those as brief as 15 minutes, can significantly impact stress levels and overall emotional well-being.

- **Stretching**: Regular stretching routines not only improve flexibility but also serve as moments of mindfulness, allowing you to connect with your body and release tension. Integrating stretching into morning or evening routines can serve as bookends to the day, offering a structured way to care for your physical self.

Nutrition and Mental Health

The adage "you are what you eat" holds more truth than you might realize, especially when it comes to your mental health. Nutrition plays a pivotal role in your emotional well-being, with certain foods having the power to uplift your mood, enhance your energy levels, and even stabilize your thoughts:

- **Omega-3 Fatty Acids**: Found in fish like salmon, walnuts, and flaxseeds, omega-3s are champions for brain health and linked to improved mood and cognitive function.

- **Whole Grains**: Foods like oatmeal, brown rice, and whole wheat bread help stabilize blood sugar levels, which can influence mood and energy throughout the day.

- **Leafy Greens**: Spinach, kale, and other green vegetables are rich in folate, a vitamin that plays a role in serotonin production, often called the "feel-good" neurotransmitter.

- **Berries**: Packed with antioxidants, berries can help reduce inflammation and stress, contributing to physical and mental health.

Incorporating these foods into your diet is not about strict regimens or denying yourself the pleasures of eating but about adding to your plate and introducing a variety of mood-boosting foods that can uplift your spirits while nourishing your body.

Seeking Professional Guidance

While personal efforts toward physical wellness can yield significant benefits, there are times when professional guidance becomes necessary. Understanding when and how to seek this help ensures that your journey towards holistic health remains safe and effective:

- **Chronic Physical Conditions**: If you are dealing with long-term physical health issues, consulting with healthcare professionals can provide tailored advice that considers both your physical and mental health needs.

- **Nutritional Counseling**: For those looking to overhaul their diet with mental health in mind, a registered dietitian or nutritionist can offer personalized guidance, helping to craft meal plans that support both physical and emotional well-being.

- **Physical Therapy**: If past injuries or chronic pain are barriers to exercise, physical therapists can design programs that accommodate these limitations, ensuring that you can engage in physical activity safely and effectively.

Reaching out for professional assistance is not a sign of weakness but an acknowledgment of the complex interplay between your physical and mental health. It signifies a commitment to nurturing yourself wholly, recognizing that the path to healing from narcissistic abuse is one that encompasses the entirety of our being.

In this realm where mind and body converse, where each influences the other in a perpetual dance, we find a holistic approach to healing. In this delicate balance, it is here that you discover the power of physical wellness to transform not just your body but your mind, offering a foundation of strength and clarity upon which you can rebuild. Through simple exercises, mindful nutrition, and the wisdom to seek guidance when needed, you navigate the waters of recovery with grace, ensuring that as you heal, you do so not just in part but in whole.

Chapter 5: Financial Independence

Rebuilding Financial Health

Navigating away from the turmoil of narcissistic abuse, the road to financial independence often presents itself as a path paved with both challenges and opportunities. Here, the concept of financial health transcends mere numbers in a bank account, embodying a form of liberation and autonomy. It is the key to unlocking doors that lead away from past constraints and towards a future where choices—about where to live, how to live, and with whom to share your life—are once again in your own hands.

Financial Health as Freedom

In the wake of such profound personal upheaval, financial health emerges not merely as economic stability but as a cornerstone of freedom. It represents the ability to make life choices without financial constraint or coercion, a particularly poignant form of independence for those trapped in manipulative relationships. This newfound financial autonomy offers a buffer against uncertainty, a source of security that supports both emotional recovery and the practicalities of building a new life.

Budgeting Basics

The foundation of financial independence is a well-considered budget, a tool that, when wielded with care, can transform aspirations of financial health into reality. A budget is not a constraint but a map, guiding spending in a way that reflects one's values and priorities. Here are steps to create a budget that serves not just as a ledger but as a blueprint for financial freedom:

- **Track Your Spending**: Keep a detailed record of all expenditures for one month. This snapshot of your financial habits can reveal surprising insights into where your money goes each month.

- **Categorize Expenses**: Divide your spending into categories such as housing, groceries, utilities, entertainment, and savings. Seeing your finances segmented this way can highlight areas for adjustment.

- **Prioritize Savings**: Treat savings as a non-negotiable category, akin to rent or utilities. Even a small, consistent allocation towards savings strengthens financial security over time.

- **Set Realistic Goals**: Whether paying down debt, saving for a down payment, or building an emergency fund, clear goals can motivate adherence to your budget and track progress.

Rebuilding Credit

For many emerging from narcissistic relationships, credit scores—a critical aspect of financial health—may have suffered. Rebuilding credit is a step-by-step process that lays the groundwork for future financial stability:

- **Review Your Credit Report**: Obtain a free credit report from the major bureaus to assess where you stand. This review can also uncover errors or fraudulent accounts opened in your name.

- **Dispute Inaccuracies**: Report any discrepancies to the credit bureaus. Removing erroneous charges or accounts can have an immediate positive impact on your credit score.

- **Start Small**: Consider a secured credit card, where the credit limit is backed by a deposit. Regular, on-time payments on such cards can slowly rebuild your credit history.

- **Pay Down Balances**: High balances on existing accounts can drag your score down. Work towards paying these off, starting with the highest interest rates first.

Empowerment Through Education

Knowledge is power, and in the realm of finances, this adage holds particularly true. Educating yourself on financial matters not only equips you with the tools to manage your money effectively but also instills a sense of confidence and control over your economic future:

- **Financial Literacy Courses**: Many community colleges and online platforms offer courses on personal finance, covering topics from budgeting to investing. These resources can demystify financial concepts and strategies.

- **Read Widely**: Books, blogs, and podcasts on financial independence and personal finance offer a wealth of knowledge that can inspire and educate. Hearing others' financial journeys can provide both practical advice and a sense of camaraderie.

- **Consult Professionals**: When ready, speaking with a financial advisor can tailor general principles of personal finance to your specific situation, helping to strategize around goals like retirement savings or investment.

In the aftermath of narcissistic abuse, rebuilding your life includes redefining your relationship with money. Financial independence is both a goal and a journey, a process of learning, planning, and making choices that align with your aspirations for the future. Through budgeting, credit rebuilding, and ongoing financial education, this journey unfolds, step by step, leading towards a destination where freedom and security await.

Chapter 6: Digital Detox

Managing Social Media and Technology

In an age where our lives are intertwined with the digital world, the line between beneficial engagement and detrimental overload becomes blurred. The influence of social media and technology on mental health, particularly for those healing from narcissistic abuse, is profound. Constant exposure to curated realities can evoke feelings of inadequacy, reignite past traumas, and foster a cycle of comparison and dissatisfaction that detracts from the healing process.

Impact of Digital Overload

The barrage of notifications, the endless scroll through polished lives, and the subtle yet persistent demand for our attention can lead to a state of mental exhaustion known as digital overload. This state not only exacerbates feelings of anxiety and depression but also alienates us from our real-life experiences and connections. For survivors of narcissistic trauma, who are working to rebuild their sense of self and reality, this digital bombardment can be especially triggering, reawakening past traumas and impeding progress towards healing.

Benefits of a Digital Detox

Stepping back from the digital world, even briefly, can have a transformative effect on mental health and overall well-being. A *digital detox*, the conscious decision to reduce or eliminate digital device usage for a set period, offers a multitude of benefits:

- **Enhanced Mood**: Disconnecting from the constant flow of information helps reduce stress and anxiety, leading to improvements in mood and emotional stability.

- **Improved Sleep:** Screen time, especially before bed, can disrupt sleep patterns. A break from screens can lead to better sleep quality and duration.

- **Strengthened Real-World Connections**: Freeing up time spent online opens opportunities for in-person interactions, fostering deeper connections with family and friends.

- **Increased Productivity and Creativity**: Without the distraction of digital devices, there is more space for focused work and creative pursuits, leading to a sense of accomplishment and fulfillment.

Implementing a Digital Detox

Initiating a digital detox requires intention and planning. Here are practical tips for creating a successful detox experience:

- **Set Clear Boundaries**: Designate specific times of the day or particular days of the week as digital-free. Communicate these boundaries to friends and family to manage expectations.

- **Discover Offline Hobbies**: Reconnect with or explore new hobbies that do not involve screens. Whether it is painting, hiking, reading, or gardening, these activities provide a fulfilling and restorative break from the digital world.

- **Mindful Technology Use**: When using digital devices, do so with purpose. Avoid mindless scrolling and choose activities that add value to your day, such as listening to a podcast or following a workout video.

- **Physical Reminders**: Keep phones, tablets, and laptops out of reach during designated detox times. Physical separation makes it easier to resist the temptation to check-in.

Creating Healthy Digital Habits

Post-detox, establishing healthy, long-term digital habits ensures that technology becomes a tool for enhancement rather than a source of stress:

- **Selective Engagement**: Curate your social media feeds to follow accounts that inspire and uplift you. Limit exposure to content or individuals that evoke negative emotions or comparisons.

- **Tech-Free Zones**: Designate areas in your home, such as the bedroom or dining table, as tech-free zones to encourage presence and connection during personal or family time.

- **Notification Management**: Limit notifications to essential communications only. This reduces the constant demand for your attention and minimizes distractions.

- **Regular Check-Ins**: Periodically assess your relationship with technology. These check-ins can help you adjust your habits to ensure they align with your well-being and life goals.

In embracing a digital detox and establishing healthier digital habits, we reclaim our time, attention, and energy from the grasp of screens. This reclamation not only supports our healing journey but also enriches our lives with genuine connections, restored focus, and a renewed appreciation for the world beyond the digital.

As we close this section, we carry forward the understanding that while technology has its place in our lives, it's the moments unplugged, the time spent in self-reflection, real-world exploration, and connection that truly nourish our souls and propel our healing. With this foundation, we are better equipped to navigate the complexities of recovery, embracing each day with presence, purpose, and a heart open to the beauty of the world around us.

Now, let us move onward, carrying these tools and insights into the next phase of our journey, where self-discovery and growth await.

Part 5: Embracing Your New Life

Imagine waking up to a day that is entirely yours, a canvas blank and waiting for your colors. You have walked through a storm, and now, standing in the calm, you hold the brushes: resilience, wisdom, and newfound joy. It's time to paint your days with hues of happiness, to spot the silver linings even on cloudy days. This section is about turning those possibilities into everyday realities, about finding and nurturing joy in moments big and small.

"The privilege of a lifetime is to become who you truly are."

Carl Jung

Chapter 1: Rediscovering Joy

Cultivating Happiness Post-Trauma

Identifying Sources of Joy

Think back to a moment when you felt a spark of genuine joy. Maybe it was the warmth of sunlight on your skin, the laughter shared over a simple meal with a friend or the satisfaction of completing a crossword puzzle. These instances, often overlooked, are wellsprings of joy waiting to be tapped into. Start by making a list of activities and experiences that have brought you happiness in the past. Don't filter or judge; just note them down. Whether it's baking, hiking, playing an instrument, or gardening, these are clues to where your joy lies.

Mindfulness in Joyful Moments

Now, with your list in hand, engage in these activities mindfully. For instance, if you're baking, notice the texture of the dough, the aroma of spices, and the warmth from the oven. Mindfulness turns these actions into immersive experiences, deepening the joy they bring. It's about being fully present, letting the experience envelop you, letting go of past worries and future anxieties. This practice not only amplifies joy but also anchors you in the now, a powerful stance from which to rebuild your life.

Joy as Resistance

Viewing joy as an act of resistance redefines the narrative of your recovery. It's a declaration that despite the pain endured, you reclaim your right to happiness. Each time you choose joy, you assert your independence from the shadows of the past. It's an act of defiance against the notion that trauma defines you. Embrace small pleasures as victories, as steps towards the life you deserve.

Building a Joyful Routine

Integrating these sources of joy into your daily routine ensures that happiness is not left to chance but becomes a steady undercurrent in your life. Here is how to make joy a habit:

- **Morning Rituals**: Start your day with an activity you love. It could be a cup of coffee enjoyed in silence, a few pages of a beloved book, or a brisk walk. This sets a positive tone for the day ahead.

- **Joy Breaks**: Schedule short breaks throughout your day dedicated to joy. Ten minutes of sketching, dancing to your favorite song, or tending to your plants can rejuvenate your spirit.

- **Evening Reflection**: End your day by noting three joyful moments you experienced. This practice not only cultivates gratitude but also trains your mind to seek out joy.

Visual Element: Joy Journal Template

A downloadable template for a Joy Journal: structured with sections for morning intentions, joy breaks, and evening reflections. This tool is designed to guide you in consciously incorporating joy into your daily life.

Interactive Element: Joy Discovery Quiz

An online quiz that helps you identify activities that might bring you joy based on your interests, past pleasures, and current goals. It offers personalized suggestions to explore, encouraging you to expand your joy repertoire.

Textual Element: Real-life Examples

- **A morning ritual example**: "Every morning, I spend fifteen minutes with my sketchbook. It doesn't matter what I draw; it's about the act of creating something. This small ritual fills me with a sense of accomplishment that carries through my day."

- **A joy break example**: "During my lunch break, I step outside for a quick walk. I focus on the feel of the breeze, the sound of birds, and the rhythm of my steps. It's a brief escape that recharges me for the afternoon."

- **An evening reflection example**: "Before bed, I jot down three things that made me smile that day. It could be as simple as a delicious meal I cooked or a funny meme a friend shared. This practice helps me end my day on a positive note, focusing on the good."

Incorporating joy into your routine is not about ignoring the complexities of healing but about balancing them with moments that uplift and inspire. It is a journey of rediscovery, where you learn not just to exist but to thrive, finding happiness in the everyday, the ordinary, and the overlooked. As you weave these practices into the fabric of your life, you will find that joy, once elusive, becomes a familiar companion, lighting your path forward.

Chapter 2: Goal Setting
Designing Your Future

The canvas of your future is vast and varied, a sprawling landscape of potential that stretches as far as the eye can see. The brush in your hand, dipped in the hues of ambition and dreams, is ready to paint your tomorrows. But where do you start? The answer lies in the power of goal setting, a compass that guides your strokes, ensuring every dab and swirl contributes to the masterpiece that will be your life.

Envisioning Your Future

Before you can set goals, you must first allow yourself to dream, and envision the future with clarity and courage. This vision encompasses all facets of your life—personal growth, career achievements, and the richness of your relationships. Picture yourself a few years down the line: What are you doing? Who is by your side? How do you feel? This vision does not need to be crystal clear, but it should serve as a beacon, guiding your goal-setting process with its light.

SMART Goals

With your vision in mind, it's time to chart the course. SMART goals, a methodology grounded in specificity and practicality, serve as the map. Each goal you set should be:

- **Specific**: Clearly define what you want to achieve. A vague goal is like a nebulous cloud—pretty to look at but impossible to grasp.

- **Measurable**: Attach numbers or markers to your goal. How will you know you have reached it if you can't measure it?

- **Achievable**: Dream big but tether your dreams to reality. An impossible goal is a ship setting sail without a rudder—it is going nowhere.

- **Relevant**: Ensure your goals align with your vision. A goal that does not serve your broader picture is a detour on your journey.

- **Time-bound**: Set deadlines. A goal without a timeline is like a story without an ending—it lacks closure and satisfaction.

Overcoming Obstacles

The path to your goals is rarely a straight line. Obstacles—external and internal—will arise. Anticipating these challenges allows you to prepare, to arm yourself with strategies and a mindset that views obstacles not as roadblocks but as stepping stones. Among these, fear of failure and self-doubt are the most insidious, whispering tales of inadequacy. Counter them with self-talk that emphasizes growth and resilience. Remember, failure is not the opposite of success; it is a part of it.

Celebrating Milestones

On the journey to your goals, milestones are the rest stops, the moments to pause, reflect, and celebrate. Recognizing these achievements, no matter how small, fuels your motivation and bolsters your self-esteem. It is a reminder of how far you have come and a token of what is possible with persistence and heart. So, celebrate these victories with a ritual—a quiet moment of gratitude, a shared celebration with loved ones, or a token of acknowledgment for yourself. These celebrations weave joy into the fabric of your pursuit, making the journey as rewarding as the destination.

Through the art of goal setting, you take the reins of your future, directing the narrative of your life with intention and insight. The process becomes a dance—a step forward, a pause, a leap—each move deliberate, each step a statement of your resolve and vision. The goals you set today are the brushstrokes of tomorrow, painting a future that resonates with the depth of your dreams and the strength of your spirit.

Chapter 3: Building Resilience

Lessons in Strength and Perseverance

Defining Resilience

Resilience is not just about bouncing back from difficulties; it is about growing through them. It involves more than mere survival; it signifies a transformative process that allows us to approach future challenges with strength and wisdom. At its core, resilience is the art of navigating life's storms, learning to sail in turbulent waters with hope as our compass.

Resilience-Building Practices

To weave resilience into the fabric of our being, we can adopt several practices that reinforce our mental and emotional fortitude:

- **Cultivating a Positive Mindset**: This doesn't mean ignoring the negative but choosing to focus on the positive aspects of our lives. It is about recognizing our power to direct our attention and choose our attitude in any given set of circumstances.

- **Practicing Self-Compassion**: Being kind to yourself, especially in moments of failure or weakness, reinforces your resilience. Again, it is about treating yourself with the same kindness and understanding you would offer to a dear friend in distress.

- **Seeking Supportnot When Needed**: No one is an island, and reaching out for support is not a sign of weakness but of wisdom. Connecting with friends, family, or support groups provides a network of encouragement and understanding that can buoy you through tough times.

- **Embracing Adaptability**: Flexibility in the face of change is a hallmark of resilience. It is about being open to new ways of thinking and being willing to adjust your sails when the wind changes direction.

Learning from Setbacks

Setbacks, while challenging, are not dead ends but detours on the path of life. They are not markers of defeat but growth opportunities. You can gain invaluable lessons in patience, strength, and perseverance with each setback. By reframing your perspective, you can see these moments not as failures but as stepping stones toward your goals. The seeds of resilience are sown and nurtured in the soil of difficulty.

- **Reflect on the Lessons**: After a setback, take time to reflect on what it taught you. Did it reveal a strength you did not know you had? Did it offer insight into a personal limitation you can work on? Each lesson is a gift, wrapped in the guise of a challenge.

- **Adjust Your Approach**: Use setbacks as a feedback mechanism. What worked? What didn't? Adjusting your approach based on these insights can turn past failures into future successes.

Resilience as a Lifelong Journey

Resilience is not a badge to be earned and then forgotten. It is a quality to be cultivated, a companion to be cherished on your lifelong journey of growth and self-discovery. It requires patience, for its roots grow deep in the soil of your experiences and time, for its lessons unfold across the chapters of your life.

- **Celebrate Your Resilient Moments**: Take time to acknowledge moments when your resilience shines. Maybe it is speaking up for yourself, tackling a challenging project, or simply getting out of bed on a tough day. These moments, big and small, are testaments to your strength.

- **Continuously Nurture Your Resilience**: Like a garden, resilience needs continuous care. Keep feeding your mind with positive thoughts, your heart with compassion, and your life with meaningful connections. Keep learning, growing, and stretching the boundaries of your comfort zone.

- **Accept That Growth is Non-Linear:** The path of resilience weaves through peaks and valleys. Accepting the non-linear nature of growth helps temper your expectations and fosters a sense of peace with the process.

Resilience equips us not just to survive life's challenges but to grow from them, to transform adversity into opportunity. It teaches us that our greatest trials can forge our greatest strengths, that in the heart of difficulty lies potential for profound personal growth. With resilience as our guide, we navigate the unpredictable waters of life not as victims of our circumstances but as architects of our destiny, building a future marked by strength, perseverance, and an unwavering hope for what lies ahead.

Chapter 4: Advocacy and Awareness

Becoming a Voice for Others

When the dust settles on the battlefield of your past struggles, you stand at the threshold of a transformative realization: your voice holds power. The stories of your survival and healing, once whispered into the void, can now serve as beacons of hope and strength for others navigating similar dark waters. The act of sharing these narratives is more than a cathartic release; it is a lifeline, a beacon of solidarity.

Sharing Your Story

The decision to share your story is a profound step in the healing process. It is an affirmation of your journey, a declaration of your resilience. In speaking out, whether through blogs, books, or public speaking, you shift from a position of isolation to one of connection. Your story, rich with the lessons of survival and the promise of healing, becomes a mirror for others, reflecting both shared pain and shared hope.

- **Platforms for Sharing**: Choose a platform that resonates with you. This could be a personal blog, a podcast, or even guest appearances on panels and discussions related to overcoming trauma.

- **Focus on Impact**: When sharing, center your narrative on the journey rather than the pain. Highlight the moments of strength and the lessons learned, offering actionable insights for others.

Engaging in Advocacy

Advocacy is the bridge between personal healing and societal change. It is an active engagement in raising awareness about narcissistic abuse, aiming to shift societal perceptions and support survivors.

- **Volunteering**: Connect with organizations dedicated to domestic abuse or mental health. Offering your time and voice can amplify their efforts to support survivors and educate the public.

- **Social Media Campaigns**: Utilize social media platforms to launch or participate in campaigns highlighting narcissistic abuse's realities. Hashtags can create communities of support and awareness.

- **Community Education**: Partner with local schools, colleges, or community centers to organize workshops and talks. Education is a powerful tool in changing narratives and supporting early detection and intervention.

Safety and Boundaries in Advocacy

As you step into the role of an advocate, remember that your well-being remains paramount. Advocacy should not come at the cost of your peace or safety.

- **Protect Your Privacy**: Decide how much of your personal story you are comfortable sharing. Use pseudonyms or speak in general terms if it helps maintain your privacy and security.

- **Set Emotional Boundaries**: Be mindful of your emotional bandwidth. Engage in advocacy work in a way that is fulfilling, not draining. It is okay to take breaks and prioritize self-care.

- **Support Systems**: Maintain a strong support system. Advocacy can bring up past traumas, so having a network of friends, family, or professionals to lean on is crucial.

The Ripple Effect of Advocacy

The impact of your advocacy efforts can ripple far beyond your immediate circle, touching lives in ways you might never fully realize. Each story shared, each workshop conducted, and each campaign launched contributes to a larger wave of change.

- **Creating Safe Spaces**: Your advocacy creates spaces

where survivors feel seen and heard, fostering a sense of community and belonging.

- **Shifting Societal Perceptions**: By bringing narratives of narcissistic abuse into the public eye, you challenge misconceptions and stigma, paving the way for a more informed and empathetic society.

- **Empowering Survivors**: Your voice can inspire action and courage in others, empowering them to seek help, share their own stories, and begin their healing journeys.

In stepping into the light of advocacy and awareness, you wield your past not as a weapon but as a tool for healing, education, and change. Through the act of sharing your story, engaging in advocacy, and navigating the delicate balance of safety and openness, you contribute to a world where the shadows of narcissistic abuse are dispelled by the collective light of awareness and support. In doing so, you not only reclaim your narrative but also offer up the pen to those still finding their way, allowing them to script their own stories of survival, resilience, and hope.

Chapter 5: The Power of New Beginnings

Writing Your Next Chapter

New chapters are the blank pages of life's book, waiting for the ink of our experiences to fill them. A fresh start after enduring the trials of narcissistic abuse is both a gift and a challenge. It is an opportunity to redefine who we are on our terms, to paint the canvas of our lives with colors of our choosing. Yet, the prospect of starting anew can be daunting, tinged with the unknown and the uncertainties it brings. Here, we explore ways to embrace this change, navigate the waters of uncertainty, and draft a personal manifesto that captures our intentions for the days ahead.

Embracing Change

Change, often viewed through a lens of apprehension, is the soil in which new beginnings take root. It is a force that dismantles the old to make way for the new, pushing us beyond the boundaries of our comfort zones into realms of untapped potential. To embrace change is to accept it as an inevitable part of growth, to see it not as an end but as a beginning. It's about recognizing that the most fulfilling and meaningful experiences often come from the seeds of change we bravely plant. Here is how to embrace change positively:

- **Acknowledge Your Feelings**: It is okay to feel a mix of emotions towards change. Acknowledging these feelings is the first step towards accepting change.

- **Seek Lessons in Change**: Every change, no matter how small, comes with lessons. Look for what each change is teaching you about life, yourself, and the world around you.

- **Visualize the Positive Outcomes**: Focus on the positive aspects and opportunities that change brings. Visualization can be a powerful tool in shifting your perspective towards optimism.

Navigating Uncertainty

With new beginnings comes a natural sense of uncertainty, a fog that clouds our path forward. Yet, within this uncertainty lies the freedom to explore, experiment, and discover. Navigating this landscape requires a compass made of your core values and goals, guiding you through the haze toward your desired destination. Here are strategies to stay grounded amidst uncertainty:

- **Root Yourself in Your Values**: Your values are your North Star, guiding your decisions and actions. When faced with uncertainty, remind yourself of what truly matters to you.

- **Set Small, Achievable Goals**: Break down your larger goals into smaller, manageable tasks. Achieving these can provide a sense of progress and control, illuminating the path step by step.

- **Embrace Flexibility**: Be open to adjusting your plans as you go. Flexibility allows you to navigate changes and challenges more effectively, turning obstacles into opportunities.

Creating a Personal Manifesto

A personal manifesto is a declaration of your intentions, values, and aspirations. It is a roadmap for your new beginning, a guiding document that reflects who you are and who you aspire to be. Crafting a personal manifesto involves introspection and honesty, a deep dive into the essence of your being. Here's how to create your manifesto:

- **Reflect on Your Core Values**: Identify the principles that are non-negotiable in your life. These form the foundation of your manifesto.

- **Envision Your Ideal Future**: Imagine the life you want to lead. What does it look like? How do you feel? Use these visions to set the direction of your manifesto.

- **Declare Your Intentions**: Write down your intentions for your life. Be specific about what you want to achieve, experience, and contribute.

- **Commit to Your Aspirations**: Outline the steps you're willing to take to realize your dreams. This commitment is a pledge to yourself to pursue your goals with determination.

Your personal manifesto is a living document, one that evolves as you do. It serves as a reminder of your journey's purpose, a beacon that lights your way through the highs and lows. Refer to it often, let it guide your decisions, and allow it to inspire growth and change.

The Role of Hope

In the narrative of new beginnings, hope is the thread that weaves through every word, every intention, and every action. It's the belief in the possibility of a better tomorrow, a force that propels you forward even when the path is unclear. Hope is both a refuge and a catalyst, offering solace in moments of doubt and motivating you to take the steps toward your envisioned future. Here is how hope plays a pivotal role in new beginnings:

- **Fuel for Forward Movement**: Hope is the energy that drives us to take action, to make the changes necessary for our growth and happiness.

- **Anchor in Adversity**: During challenging times, hope serves as an anchor, reminding you of your strengths, your growth and the potential for positive change.

- **Source of Inspiration:** Hope inspires creativity and innovation, encouraging us to find new solutions and paths forward.

Cultivate hope by surrounding yourself with positivity, celebrating every victory, no matter how small, and reminding yourself of your resilience and strength. Let hope be your constant companion, guiding you through the uncertainties of new beginnings towards the fulfillment and joy that await in the chapters yet to be written.

As you navigate the intricacies of starting afresh, these pillars—embracing change, navigating uncertainty, creating a personal manifesto, and holding onto hope—serve as our guideposts. They remind you that though the journey may be fraught with challenges, it is also ripe with opportunity. With each step, you move closer to the life you envision, a life crafted by your hands, guided by your values, and illuminated by your hopes.

Chapter 6: Maintaining Your Progress

Strategies for Long-Term Success

In the dance of life, maintaining rhythm is key. This holds especially true when nurturing the seeds of growth and healing post-trauma. The tune may change, the tempo may shift, but the dance goes on. Here, we explore the choreography of maintaining progress—thoughtful steps that keep us moving forward, even when the music fades into silence.

Monitoring Progress

Keeping an eye on your stride helps ensure you are not just moving but moving in the right direction. Consider these approaches to keep track of your advancement:

- **Reflective Journaling**: Unlike traditional journaling, which captures daily events, reflective journaling focuses on your feelings, reactions, and the lessons learned. It's a mirror showing not just where you have been but how you have grown.

- **Regular Check-Ins**: Dedicate a time each week for self-assessment. Look back at what you have accomplished, and what has been challenging, and adjust your actions accordingly. It is like pausing to read a map during a journey, ensuring you're still on the path you set out to follow.

- **Feedback Loops**: Constructive input from those you trust can be illuminating. Sometimes, they see your progress more clearly than you can. Engage in open conversations with close friends, family, or mentors about your growth. It's akin to having a coach in your corner, offering insights to refine your technique.

Adapting to Change

The only constant in life is change. Embracing this truth allows us to remain fluid, to flow with life's ebbs and flows rather than resist them.

- **Stay Open**: When plans do not unfold as expected, view it as an opportunity to explore new avenues rather than a setback. It is like improvising in jazz; the unexpected notes often add the most beauty.

- **Adjust Goals**: Goals are important, but they should not be rigid. If a goal no longer serves you or seems out of reach, tweak it. This is not about lowering standards but aligning your aspirations with your evolving self.

- **Embrace Learning**: Every misstep is a lesson in disguise. Instead of wallowing in frustration, ask yourself, "What can this teach me?" This mindset turns obstacles into stepping stones.

Self-Care as Maintenance

The journey of healing and growth is a marathon, not a sprint. Self-care is the water station along the route, a necessary stop to replenish and nurture ourselves.

- **Mind, Body, Spirit**: Self-care encompasses more than bubble baths and spa days. It involves tending to your emotional well-being, keeping your body healthy, and feeding your spirit. Activities like meditation, exercise, and engaging in hobbies that light you up are integral.

- **Boundaries**: Learning to say "*No*" is a supreme form of self-care. It protects your energy and ensures you're only engaging in activities and relationships that support your well-being.

- **Routine**: Incorporate self-care into your daily routine. Make it as non-negotiable as brushing your teeth. Consistency in self-care is what sustains us through the marathon.

Seeking Support When Needed

No man is an island, and no one should navigate the waters of healing and growth in solitude. Support is the lighthouse guiding you through foggy nights.

- **Professional Help**: Therapists, counselors, and coaches can offer expert guidance tailored to your needs. They are like navigators in uncharted waters, helping you steer clear of rocks and find the best currents to ride.

- **Community**: Support groups, both in-person and on-line, connect you with others who understand your struggles. They are a reminder that you are not alone in your journey and that others are also crossing the same vast sea.

- **Vulnerability**: Opening up about your needs can be daunting, but also deeply powerful. Vulnerability invites connection, understanding, and the kind of support that truly makes a difference.

In this dance of life, maintaining progress requires attentiveness, flexibility, self-nurturing, and the courage to reach out for support. It is about knowing when to step forward, when to pause, and when to lean on others. With these strategies in hand, the dance goes on, not just as a sequence of steps but as an expression of growth, resilience, and the joy of moving to your own rhythm.

Chapter 7: Celebrating You

Acknowledging Your Journey and Achievements

The path you are walking will be marked by moments of courage, profound self-discovery, and instances where you stood firm even when the ground seemed to tremble beneath your feet. It is these milestones that deserve recognition, a pause in the relentless march of days to honor how far you have come. This chapter unfolds as a tribute to you, a celebration of the resilience and strength that's been both your armor and your compass.

Recognizing Your Strength

Take a moment to reflect on the obstacles you have navigated, the challenges you have overcome, and the growth that has been both the journey and the destination. Think about the times you chose to move forward, even when shadows obscured the path. These moments, these choices, are testaments to a strength that deserves not just acknowledgment but celebration. You have shown an incredible resilience that's not just about surviving but transforming adversity into growth. Acknowledge this strength, not as a fleeting trait but as a core part of who you are.

Celebration as Ritual

Marking milestones and achievements with personal rituals infuses your journey with a sense of sacredness. These rituals, whether simple or elaborate, act as markers of progress, creating tangible memories of the moments you choose to honor. Consider lighting a candle each time you overcome a challenge, writing a letter to yourself to commemorate a milestone, or planting a tree in honor of your growth. These acts of celebration not only acknowledge your achievements but also embed them in your memory, serving as beacons during times when the path ahead seems daunting.

Gratitude for the Journey

Gratitude turns what we have into enough and more. It shifts the focus from what is missing to the present abundance. Embrace gratitude for your journey, for both the highs and the lows. Each step, each stumble, has been a part of shaping you into the person you are today. Writing down three things you are grateful for at the end of each day can transform your perspective, highlighting the progress and beauty in your journey. This practice nurtures a positive outlook, reinforcing the idea that even in hardship, *there's always something to be thankful for.*

Inspiring Others

Your journey, marked by its unique trials and triumphs, can be a source of inspiration for others walking a similar path. Sharing your story, whether in intimate gatherings or through broader platforms, does more than validate your experiences—it offers hope. It reminds others that healing is possible, that thriving is achievable, and that they are not alone in their struggles. Your achievements, celebrated openly, become a lighthouse for those still navigating through the storm, offering guidance and encouragement.

The tapestry of your experiences, woven with threads of resilience, strength, and growth, stands as a testament to your journey. It is a narrative that deserves to be celebrated, not just in grand gestures but in everyday acknowledgments of your progress. These celebrations, rituals, and expressions of gratitude not only enrich your path but also light the way for others, spreading ripples of hope and inspiration.

As we close this section, remember that every step taken, every obstacle overcome, and every moment of self-discovery contributes to the rich, complex tapestry of your life. These achievements, both big and small, are milestones on your path, deserving of recognition and celebration. They remind you of your strength, your resilience, and your capacity for growth. By honoring your journey and sharing your story, you not only affirm your progress but also inspire others to believe in the possibility of transformation. This narrative of celebration and gratitude weaves through the tapestry of healing, highlighting the beauty in our experiences and the strength within us all. As we move forward, let us carry this spirit of celebration and hope into every new chapter, embracing each step with courage and an open heart.

Conclusion

As we stand at the threshold of this journey's end, we must pause and reflect on the profound voyage we've undertaken together. From the shadowed valleys of narcissistic trauma to the empowering peaks of healing, growth, and renewal, this path has been anything but linear. It is a testament to the resilience of the human spirit, *your spirit*, a narrative that speaks volumes of your courage to step into the light from the darkest places.

In these pages, we have traversed the rugged terrain of understanding narcissistic abuse, armed with the compass of self-compassion—a vital tool that has illuminated your path. This journey underscored the transformative power of treating yourself with the same kindness and empathy you would offer a dear friend, helping us to gently dismantle the fortress of self-criticism and nurture a loving relationship with yourself.

We have underscored the importance of establishing clear boundaries and the indispensable role of self-care, highlighting practices like mindfulness, journaling, and physical wellness. These are not mere strategies but lifelines that anchor us in the tumultuous seas of recovery, ensuring we remain steadfast in our commitment to our well-being.

Empowerment has been a beacon on this journey, shining brightly through the darkness. By educating ourselves about narcissistic abuse and embracing supportive communities, we've transformed our pain into a powerful catalyst for change. This empowerment has not only fortified us but has also spurred us to advocate for awareness and support for others navigating similar paths.

I have urged you to view healing not as a destination but as a continuous journey of personal development, learning, and self-discovery. This perspective opens up a world of possibilities, where each step, each misstep, and every victory contributes to the rich tapestry of your life.

Now, as you turn these insights into action, remember the potential for transformation and renewal that lies within you. Share your stories, lend your voice to the chorus of those advocating for change, and let the lessons learned be a beacon for others. Your strength and resilience in facing past traumas are nothing short of remarkable. Your journey, with all its ups and downs, is a powerful narrative of hope and empowerment.

As we part ways on this written journey, I extend my heartfelt gratitude to you for allowing me to be a part of your healing process. The courage it takes to confront and move beyond narcissistic abuse cannot be overstated. I stand with you in solidarity, committed to supporting and uplifting others as they navigate their paths to recovery and empowerment.

In closing, remember that despite the challenges and setbacks you may encounter, a fulfilling life beyond narcissistic abuse is within your reach. Embrace your new beginnings with open arms and an open heart. The future is ripe with opportunities for growth, joy, and fulfillment.

Thank you for embarking on this journey with me. Here's to your continued healing, growth, and empowerment. Remember, you are not alone. Together, we move forward into a future bright with promise and hope.

With gratitude and solidarity,

Graham

Shine A Light for Others to Follow

You've just finished "The Narcissistic Trauma Survival Guide" by Graham Michaels, equipped with the knowledge to heal from narcissistic abuse. Now, you have the chance to light the way for others by sharing your experience.

Your honest review on Amazon can guide fellow survivors to this essential resource, offering them hope and a path forward. It's a powerful way to pass on the support you've found.

Simply scan this code!

Thank you for helping to extend a lifeline to those still navigating their journey to recovery. Your words make a world of difference, keeping the spirit of healing and empowerment alive for everyone touched by narcissistic trauma.

References

- Charlie Health. (2024). The long-term effects of narcissistic abuse. https://www.charliehealth.com/post/the-long-term-effects-of-narcissistic-abuse

- Medical News Today. (2024). What is gaslighting? Examples and how to respond. https://www.medicalnewstoday.com/articles/gaslighting

- Sabino Recovery. (2024). What does a trauma bond with a narcissist look like? https://www.sabinorecovery.com/what-does-a-trauma-bond-with-a-narcissist-look-like

- Cleveland Clinic. (2023). CPTSD (Complex PTSD): What it is, symptoms & treatment. https://my.clevelandclinic.org/health/diseases/24881-cptsd-complex-ptsd

- Talkspace. (2023). How to leave & end a relationship with a narcissist. https://www.talkspace.com/mental-health/conditions/articles/how-to-leave-a-narcissist/

- Choosing Therapy. (2023). Going no contact with a narcissist: Everything you need to know. https://www.choosingtherapy.com/no-contact-with-a-narcissist/

- Psych Central. (2022). The grey rock method: A technique for handling toxic people. https://psychcentral.co m/health/grey-rock-method

- Nussbaum Family Law. (2023). Legal help for narcissistic abuse. https://nussbaumlaw.ca/legal-help-narcissisti c-abuse/

- Psychology Today. (2021). 6 science-based self-compassion exercises. https://www.psychologytoday.com/us/blog/click-here -happiness/202101/6-science-based-self-compassion-exe rcises

- Verywell Health. (2023). How to set healthy boundaries with anyone. https://www.verywellhealth.com/set ting-boundaries-5208802

- Mayo Clinic. (2023). Narcissistic personality disorder - Symptoms and causes. https://www.mayoclinic.org/diseases-conditions/narciss istic-personality-disorder/symptoms-causes/syc-203666 62

- Verywell Mind. (2023). How to find a narcissistic abuse support group. https://www.verywellmind.com/how-t o-find-a-narcissistic-abuse-support-group-5271477

- National Institutes of Health. (2018). Mindfulness-based treatments for posttraumatic stress disorder. https://ww w.ncbi.nlm.nih.gov/pmc/articles/PMC5547539/

- Day One. (2023). Emotional journaling: How to use journaling to process emotions. https://dayoneapp.com/blog/emotional-journaling

- ABC News. (2013). Art therapy saves a schizophrenic hit by two cars. https://abcnews.go.com/Health/art-therap y-saves-schizophrenic-hit-cars/story?id=19507297

- National Institutes of Health. (2020). Nutrition and fitness: Mental health. https://www.ncbi.nlm.nih.gov/pm c/articles/PMC7353309/

- Develop Good Habits. (2023). 35 SMART goals examples for all areas of your life. https://www.developgoodh abits.com/smart-goals-examples/

- White Swan Foundation. (2016). After abuse: Building resilience for better emotional health. https://www.whiteswanfoundation.org/life-stages/child hood/after-abuse-building-resilience-for-better-emotion al-health

Made in United States
Troutdale, OR
04/23/2024

19383192R00096